Circular Walks
on the Tuscany-Umbria border

Cortona • Trasimeno • Niccone Valley

Umbertide • Montone • Perugia

Martin Daykin

ISBN 0-9548634-0-2

Printed by Tipografia Gamma, Città di Castello, Italy

Front Cover: Torre di Fiume (In the Pian di Marte)

Contents

Introduction

The area between *Cortona* and *Umbertide* on the Tuscan-Umbrian border offers some excellent walking opportunities. I moved here in spring 1999 and after spending a year restoring a farmhouse, I began to explore the area on foot. I love to walk in such a beautiful landscape and am fascinated by the history that has shaped it. Ancient roads cross the hillsides, abandoned terracing is now overgrown with thick woodland and many old buildings, both ruinous and restored, are dotted all over the countryside. The castles in this border area are an indication that this was a highly fought over territory; it has not always been the peaceful rural idyll that it is today.

I decided to write this book after trying to use other walking guides. Many of the walks were linear and nearly all lacked sufficient detail to keep you on the right path. With this book I hope to overcome several drawbacks for the walker in this area. The walks are circular (with the exception of *Passignano* to *Terontola*), this avoids having to take two cars or relying on public transport to get back, a good idea in theory, but the practice can involve hours of waiting. Sign posting is haphazard or non-existent on many routes and good maps are hard to find. I hope that my descriptions and maps are detailed enough so that you can always be sure of where to go. Of course, changes occur all the time and I cannot accept responsibilty if you get lost, however, I do try to keep updates posted on the website and if you come across changes please let me know. You can contact me via the website **www.tuscanyumbriawalks.com**.

I have given walking times between junctions and landmarks; this is based on my walking speed and refers only to the time walking. I am reasonably young and fit and walk alone. Obviously, a group will be chatting, stopping to read the directions and to look at things along the way. Read the directions with this in mind and be prepared to spend longer on a walk than my stated time. A big group, or slow walkers should allow at least 15 minutes in addition to every hour of my walking time.

Thanks

I'd like to thank all those who have suggested walking routes and tested my instructions; everyone who has bought this book; Stefania Serpi and Marion Rauschenberger, the translators for the German and Italian versions; but most of all Emma, my wife, for all her help and encouragement.

1 Useful Information

1.1 Map of the area

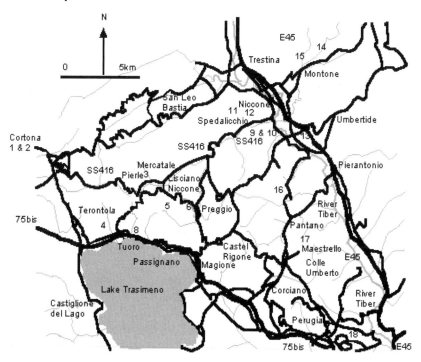

Key to Maps

———————————————— Footpath

———————————————— Track

━━━━━━━━━━━━━━━━ Tarmac Road

▬▬▬▬▬▬▬▬▬▬▬▬ Dual Carriageway

Paths and roads not on the route are shown in grey:

———————————————— Footpath

———————————————— Track

━━━━━━━━━━━━━━━━ Tarmac Road

▬▬▬▬▬▬▬▬▬▬▬▬ Dual Carriageway

Water is shown in a lighter gray:

∼∼∼∼∼∼∼∼∼∼∼∼ River

- - - - - - - - - - - - - - - - - Railway (only on Passignano-Terontola walk)

1.2 When to walk

The best months for walking in this area are January to May and September to October. January and February can be bitingly cold and there may be snow occasionally. However, many days have bright blue skies and if you wear warm clothing (thermal underwear really helps), if the conditions are right it is a wonderful time of year to walk.

The weather in March and April is hard to predict, it can be warm and sunny, there may be a late wintry blast with the higher peaks dusted in snow, or there might be typical April showers and even thunderstorms. In late April and May; you are treated to an amazing wildflower display; by late May and June, it is worth setting off early to avoid the higher temperatures later on in the day.

If you wish to walk in the height of summer, I would recommend setting off very early with plenty of water, sunblock and a hat. In the summer and especially the autumn, an early morning fog sometimes covers the *Niccone Valley*. As you climb, you have the amazing sight of a thick blanket of fog stretched out below you, often, by the time you return, the fog has lifted and it is a bright sunny day.

In late September and October, you can enjoy a riot of autumn colours across the hillsides; temperatures start to drop and the number of rainy days increases. There is nothing to stop you walking in November and December, however it is advisable to have alternatives planned in case of rain. Given the wealth of art treasures and medieval towns in the area, this should not be a problem.

1.3 Where to stay

Gorgacce Rentals specialise in holiday rental properties in the area covered by this book. My parents-in-law, David and Dilys Cordingley, have run the agency since 1990 and offer a wide range of houses and apartments. For more information, try their user-friendly web-site **www.tuscanyumbria.com**.

1.4   What to take

Good walking boots are highly recommended. Outside the summer months, many paths can be muddy and the hilly landscape means that steep ascents and descents are unavoidable on circular walks. I have recently discovered walking poles; high-tech telescopic walking sticks, these can assist greatly on steep climbs and take the weight off your knees when descending. A compass can be useful to align yourself when map reading and picking out landmarks. If you have come unprepared, hunting and fishing shops are a good source of equipment and large sport shops also sell walking boots. A loud whistle is a good way of letting hunters know you are around.

The maps in the book should be sufficient to get you around each route but if you need more detail, some good walking maps of the *Upper Tiber Valley* are available (Percorsi Verdi Alta Valle del Tevero Umbro). I bought mine at the Gulliver bookshop just off the main square in *Umbertide's* centro storico. You can also buy large-scale military maps at this shop.

The sun is strong even in spring and autumn, so use sun block and wear a hat and sunglasses. Take water even in winter, (lots in hot weather) and for any walk over 2 hours, take some chocolate or dried fruit to give yourself an energy boost. Take a mobile phone, especially if you are walking alone (try and have an English/Italian speaker's number with you if you don't talk Italian). On some walks I have recommended taking secateurs, in the spring plants grow rapidly and paths can become overgrown. Secateurs are available at ironmongers (ferramenta) and garden supply shops. If you don't have any, you will have to hope that the hordes of people who have already bought this book will have cut back the undergrowth for you.

1.5   Emergency numbers

112 Carabinieri (Police); 113 any emergency service; 115 Fire Brigade; 116 for road assistance (if you have a hire car, telephone the rental company); and 118 Ambulance. Although this is a low crime area, it is never wise to leave your car parked with valuables left inside, don't put items in the car that you aren't going to take on the walk.

1.6 Hunting

The hunting season starts in September and continues through to January. Occasionally, a whole hillside can be closed when a wild boar hunt takes place. Otherwise, the hunters roam in small groups and shoot any animal or bird they come across.

Most hunting takes place at weekends, so it may be advisable to plan a different activity. The walk up *Monte Tezio* is in a nature reserve and in theory avoids this problem. When I see a group of men in camouflage, I whistle loudly (avoiding bird impressions!). If you are in a group, strike up a loud conversation. When hunting is taking place nearby make your presence known. In *Umbria*, Wednesdays and Fridays are the days when hunting is not permitted.

1.7 Wildlife

Given the locals' fondness for hunting, the wildlife is unsurprisingly, quite shy. There are deer, wild boar, foxes, porcupines, pine martens, hares and badgers amongst others. They will all keep out of your way and if you do see any, you can count yourself lucky. Look out for wild boar tracks in soft ground and for patches of disturbed soil that they have rooted through in search of food.

Many people worry a great deal about snakes; do not allow yourself to become overly anxious about them. You are far more likely to see a harmless grass snake than a viper. A grass snake is long and green, sometimes with a brown pattern on its back. A viper is small and dark brown with diamond markings and an angular head. Look them up on the Internet if you want to see pictures.

Wear walking boots and in long grass, use a stick to scare snakes away. In the very unlikely event of snakebite, remain calm and go to hospital as quickly as possible. Remember, a bite from a viper is very rarely life threatening. If you find yourself worrying unduly, walk at the back of your group, any snakes will have been scared away by the others in front of you! In case you are wondering, I have only seen one viper while researching this book. Small suction pumps are available from chemists (farmacia) and are used to draw the venom from a bite.

1.8 Dogs

Many Italian houses have guard dogs; fortunately they are usually behind fences or tied up. Carry a walking stick if dogs make you nervous. Most of the locals are wary of the white sheepdogs known as Maremanno. I have often been barked at but never attacked by the dogs I have encountered on these walks. If you are walking with a dog, watch out for livestock. Between February and the start of September always keep your dog on a lead; the illegal practice of putting out poisoned bait for foxes and other animals is still widespread.

1.9 Restaurants

Tuscany and *Umbria* are famous for their simple cooking styles, which use high quality local ingredients to give the food its wonderful taste. Sitting down to a good meal is a great way to finish a day's walking and prices are generally very reasonable. There are lots of excellent restaurants in the area so don't be afraid to try a place I haven't recommended.

Cortona:

Cortona is a very busy tourist town and it is always advisable to book a table in advance. There are plenty of restaurants and most of them are good, many are closed on Tuesdays. My favourite is *Fufluns*, located just off the *Piazza Signorelli*, it's great value for money but there is no view. If you want a light lunch, *La Saletta* on the *Via Nazionale* is a good bet.

Fufluns ☎ 0575 604140 (moderate) Trattoria and pizzeria. Great antipasti.
La Saletta (no booking required). Snacks, primi piatti

In the Niccone Valley:

Lisciano Niccone
Il Ristorante da Gianna ☎ 075 844358 (moderate) Pizzeria and trattoria.
Pizzeria da Giuliano, (Fizz Bar) ☎ 075 844124 (inexpensive) Pizzeria and trattoria.

Mercatale
Trattoria Mimmi ☎ 0575 619029 (moderate) Fixed menu. Lots of fresh homemade pasta.

Sorbello di Sant'Andrea
Le Capannine di Sommavilla ☎ 0575 638112 (moderate) Organic and vegetarian unless meat ordered in advance. (Also Sunday breakfast/brunch from 9.30am)

Spedalicchio (follow signs to Bastia Creti from the village)
Calagrana ☎ 075 941 0865 (moderate) Great food, Italian restauranters who have recently moved back from the UK.

Molino Vitelli
La Chiusa ☎ 075 941 0774 / 941 0848 (expensive). One of Italy's top TV cooks makes her own Umbrian dishes with a Croatian flavour, all organic.
Cantina Girasole ☎ 075 9410798 (moderate) Niccone valley vineyard with its own restaurant; excellent organic beef.

Niccone
Nonna Gelsa ☎ 075 9410699 (moderate) Excellent Umbrian cooking.

Umbertide:

La Rocca ☎ 075 9411828 (moderate/expensive). Fish a speciality
Appennino ☎ 3343536585 (moderate) More excellent Umbrian cooking with a view over the Tiber.
Orchestra (moderate) Wine bar / restaurant in the main square
Habernero ☎ 0759415744 (moderate) Underground pizzeria in the old part of town.
Gildo ☎ 075 9413542 (moderate) restaurant / pizzeria on the road to Preggio from Umbertide (4 km).

Montone:

Del Verziere ☎ 075 9306512 (moderate)
Erbe Luna ☎ 075 9306405 (moderate)

Perugia:

I haven't been lucky enough to have a really good meal in Perugia yet. However, I've been told that there are many good restaurants including: *La Lanterna* on *Via U. Rocchi*, ☎ 075 5726 397 (expensive) and *Osteria il Gufo* on *Via della Viola*, ☎ 075 5732511 (inexpensive). Another recommendation I've had is the *Pizzeria Mediterraneo*, somewhere near the *Duomo* (Cathedral).

2 The Walks

2.1 Cortona walk (allow 1 hour 45 minutes)

Walking time: 1 hour 20 minutes. Fairly easy, but a steep descent.

Cortona is an ancient town dating back to Etruscan times. Look in the lower parts of the town walls and you can still see the huge blocks of stone that the Etruscan wall was built from. Apart from the property and tourism boom that the town is currently undergoing, its heyday was in the medieval period from around 1100 to 1400. During this era,

Cortona was an independent city-state and its grandest buildings date back to this time. Later, it was a Florentine outpost on the border with the city-state of *Perugia* and then the Papal States. A combination of high taxation and under-investment left the centre in a medieval time warp. There are two fine Renaissance churches outside the walls but very little architecture from this period within the town.

To Find The Start

Park in one of the car parks outside the town walls, these can be full during the tourist season so it's best to arrive early. The walk begins in the *Piazza della Repubblica*

Palazzo Comunale and the Piazza della Repubblica

in the centre of *Cortona*. The most impressive building in the square (and the town) is the medieval town hall, the *Palazzo Communale*, which dates back to the 1200's.

Walk synopsis

(A) Leave the centre of *Cortona* and go through the park.

(B) Climb from near the tennis courts to *Torreone*, a hamlet at the top of the town, then go along a track to the church of *Santa Margherita*.

(C) A quick detour from *Santa Margherita* up to the *Medici Fortress* then down to the *Piazza Signorelli* through steep medieval streets.

(D) A view from the cathedral wall, then more narrow medieval streets before returning to the start **(A)**.

Walk 1: Cortona

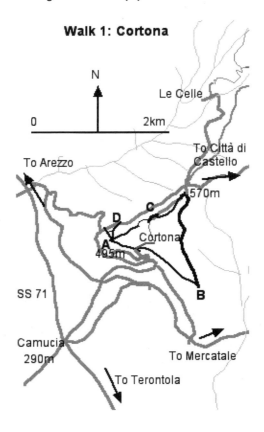

Start (A)

0:00   In the *Piazza della Repubblica*, stand with your back to the steps which lead up to the *Palazzo Communale*, and walk along *Via Nazionale*; this is the street at the right corner (east) of the Piazza. After 3 minutes, you should be at the end of the street, ignore *Via Santa Margherita* going up to the left. The flagstone-paved street finishes and joins a tarmac road on a sharp bend.

0:03   Continue straight on, ignoring the road descending to the right near a war memorial. A minute later, you pass the church of *San Domenico* on your left. There is a badly damaged fresco by Fra Angelico behind glass above the entrance door. Just after the church, turn left into the public gardens. You pass another war memorial and then a fountain on the right. A minute later, there is a play area on the left.

0:05   Continue straight on, there are great views of the *Val di Chiana* and *Lake Trasimeno* from here. Every tree that lines the road represents a person from the area killed in World War I and II. As you can see, the loss of life was considerable. 13 minutes from the play area, the gravel ends. On your left there are some indoor tennis courts **(B)**.

0:18   Follow the tarmac road around to the left, and continue straight on, climbing steadily. The road is not busy but it is a sensible pre-caution to walk on the left so that you face any oncoming traffic. 3 minutes after joining the tarmac, the road is lined with cypress-es. You pass several houses on the way up, after 15 minutes you pass *Bramasole*, the house that featured in the book "Under the Tuscan Sun". It is covered in orange/yellow stucco and has a madonnina set in the wall.

0:36   After another 8 minutes, you arrive at the junction at the top. There is a bar on your left, it's a good spot to refresh yourself after the climb (closed Wednesdays). Turn left here and after a minute turn left again onto the cypress-lined track (sign posted with red and white markers by the Club Alpini Italia (CAI)). After 3 minutes, the track curves sharply right and a tarmac road heads off to the left.

0:48 Continue along the track and after 8 minutes, you join a tarmac road (this is further along the road that you were on when you first joined the track). Turn left onto the road; go through the city walls, and a minute later, you are in front of the church of *Santa Margherita* **(C)**. Avoid using the bar here; the owner has a tendency to charge tourists higher prices than those shown on the list.

0:57 Take a quick detour up to the *Medici Fortress* (which was also the site of the Etruscan fortress), this is often shut, but the view from up here makes the short walk worthwhile. Facing the church, take the path going up diagonally to your left. Just before you get to the fortress, take a small path on your left, 3 minutes from *Santa Margherita* you should be standing on a level piece of ground with a fantastic panoramic view.

1:00 Return the way you came (3 minutes) and cross the square, keeping the facade of the church on your left. Go through the gap in the balustrade and turn right down a cobbled path. 3 minutes later, the path emerges onto a street at the top of Cortona. Turn left and then right (straight on), there is a small church on your right. A minute later, you come to a square with ilex trees (it is actually shaped like a triangle), turn right and head down the incredibly steep *Via Berretini*.

1:07 A minute later, you pass the house of the painter and architect Pietro da Cortona (Pietro Berretini 1596-1669) on your right. Immediately after, you pass a large medieval water cistern on your left. Continue down for another 2 minutes and you pass the church of *San Francesco* on the left, the first Franciscan church to be built outside *Assisi*.

1:10 Immediately after, go straight over the crossroads and down the pedestrian *Via Santucci*. 2 minutes later, you are at the bottom; continue straight on and you are back in the *Piazza della Repubblica* **(A)**. You may feel that it's time for refreshments in one of the bars, if not, continue with the walk.

1:12 Pass to the right of the *Palazzo Communale* and a minute later you are in *Piazza Signorelli*. Here, you will find the entrance to the *Etruscan Museum* (*Museo dell' Accademia Etrusca*). The museum houses the Etruscan artefacts found in the area, a collection of paintings and Egyptian mummies. It is well worth a look around, but if you are really interested in the Etruscans, see if you can join a guided tour. You can also arrange visits to the Etruscan tombs in the plain below *Cortona*, where many of the pieces on display were found.

1:13   Exit the Piazza down *Via Casale* (follow signs to the *Cattedrale*), cross *Piazza G. Franciolini*, into *Piazza del Duomo*. 2 minutes from *Piazza Signorelli* you should be admiring the view from the wall on the edge of *Piazza del Duomo* **(D)**.

1:14   Turn around, on your left is the *Duomo* (Cathederal) and on your right, the *Museo Diocesano*, which displays art works from *Cortona's* churches. (Shut Mondays and open 10.00-19.00 from April to October; 10.00-17.00 in other months). The *Duomo* is only for serious church enthusiasts, but the small *Museo Diocesano* contains a wonderful altarpiece depicting the annunciation by Fra Angelico. It also has a couple of paintings by Luca Signorelli, the most famous painter from Cortona and a rather gloomy canvas by Pietro da Cortona, whose house you walked past earlier.
Walk down *Via Zefferini* at the far right of *Piazza del Duomo*, take the first right onto *Via Cioli* and turn left onto a narrow street with overhanging houses, *Via Ianelli*. This is how much of Cortona would have looked; the overhangs were removed from most houses to allow light into the narrow streets. It is now 3 minutes from the wall on the edge of *Piazza del Duomo*.

1:17   At the end of *Via Ianelli*, you can turn left up *Via Roma*, which will take you back to the *Piazza della Repubblica* **(A)** in 3 minutes. Alternatively, you can turn right onto *Via Roma* and then immediately left along the town wall. Lose yourself in the maze of narrow streets running up from the wall; as long as you keep going up, you will eventually arrive back at the square.

Walking time: 1:20

2.2   Above Cortona (allow over 4 hours)

Walking time: 3 hours 20 minutes Steep in places, some rough terrain, one section can be overgrown, take secateurs.

Much of this walk is through woods, and I would advise taking the extension along the ridge at the top if you want to enjoy panoramic views. Take secateurs if you intend to take the extension as it can be overgrown with brambles in one place. The majority of the ascent uses the route of the Roman road to *Città di Castello*. It was used by St. Francis when travelling between *Cortona* and *La Verna*; the Franciscan retreat high above *Arezzo* where he received the stigmata. On the return route, you can make a quick visit to *Le Celle*, the Franciscan retreat in the hills near *Cortona*.

To Find The Start

This walk starts at the car park outside the church of *Santa Margherita*. To find it by car, follow signs to *Città di Castello* from *Cortona*, and when you reach the hamlet of *Torreone* take a right for *Santuario di Santa Margherita*. If you approach *Cortona* on the road from *Città di Castello*, the turning will be on the left before you arrive at the town.

Walk 2: Above Cortona

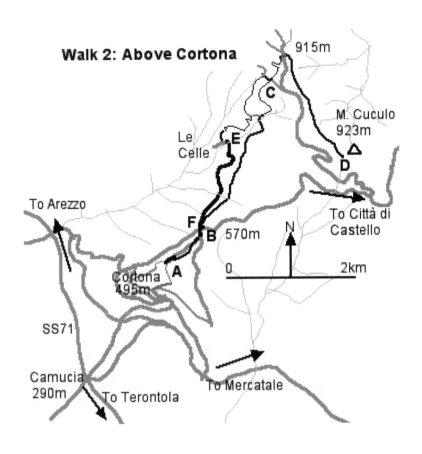

Walk Synopsis

(A) Leave *Santa Margherita* and follow a cypress-lined track to *Torreone*.

(B) The track starts to climb and then becomes paved with Roman flagstones.

(C) For a panoramic view take the extension up to and along the ridge.

(D) From the panoramic saddle, retrace your steps to **(C)** and then descend through the woods until you come to the tarmac road.

(E) Walk along the tarmac road to the junction at **(F)**.

(F) A very short walk and you arrive at **(B)**. Retrace your steps to the start **(A)**.

Start (A)

0:00 Walk out through the city walls from the car park. Almost imme-diately afterwards, take the cypress lined track on the right marked with red and white by the Club Alpini Italia (CAI). 9 min-utes from the car park the path curves sharply left. Ignore the tarmac road on the right, which leads towards the *Medici Fortress*.

0:09 After another 4 minutes, you rejoin the tarmac road that you set out on. Turn right onto the road, ignore a track on the left and a road on the right and a minute later you arrive at a crossroads. This is the hamlet of *Torreone*; the *Hotel Corys* is on your right and there is a church straight ahead **(B)**. Cross the road in front of you and take the track passing just to the left of the church. This is marked as CAI path 561.

0:14 Continue past several houses, the path is still marked with CAI signs for path 561. After 4 minutes a path merges from the left, continue straight on. 8 minutes after this, the road forks. Turn left and you pass a madonnina. Look back to your left and there is a lovely view of *Cortona* and the *Val di Chiana*. 8 minutes after the shrine, you pass the grassy drive to a house high up on the right hand side. To the left are more views of the *Val di Chiana*.

0:34 4 minutes later, you pass a second drive to the house. A minute later, the road is laid with flagstones. This is the start of the Roman road to *Città di Castello*. 4 minutes from the start of the paving, the main track takes a sharp left. Continue straight on the narrower path, still marked CAI 561.

0:43 Now the path enters a pine wood. 3 minutes after the fork, the path takes a sharp right going uphill, and 3 minutes later you come to a large clearing. The slope here is a mixture of rock and heather. Follow the path along to the left; it then winds up through the clearing. 9 minutes later you come to a fork; take the flagstone path up to the right. 7 minutes later, you emerge onto an unpaved road **(C)**. If you do not wish to take the extension up to the ridge, turn left onto the road (CAI path 563) and ignore the following section.

1:05 **Extension (this adds 70 minutes of walking time)**
Go straight over the unpaved road and take a path entering the wood to your left. The path is still marked CAI 561. 5 minutes later, the path emerges from the wood, there are springs on this slope and the ground is wet and boggy. You may need to get your secateurs out at this point; the abundant water allows the plants to grow quickly here. Watch out, the flagstones can be slippery as a result of the water constantly flowing over them.

1:10 6 minutes after leaving the wood you arrive at a tarmac road. There is a war memorial here and a picnic area. Turn left onto the tarmac and then immediately right onto a track marked CAI 50. This track runs along the ridge and the objective is a panoramic saddle with views of the *Val di Chiana* and *Lake Trasimeno*.

1:16 9 minutes after joining the path, you come to a fork; take the higher right hand track. CAI 50 markers continue to sign the way. 4 minutes later follow the main path as it curves left; two minor paths join diagonally from behind and in front on the right. After another 2 minutes, the track curves right in a clearing; ignore a track joining diagonally from behind on the left. 7 minutes later the roof of a house is visible below on the right and 2 minutes after this you arrive at the panoramic saddle **(D)**.

1:40 There are views to both sides, particularly to the right (SSW). On a clear day, you should see *Lake Trasimeno*, the *Val di Chiana* and the *Medici Fortress*, just above the starting point of the walk. Return the way you came and 35 minutes later, you should be back at the unpaved road. Turn right here **(C)**.
End of extension

2:15/1:05 Continue down the road, it is marked as CAI path 563. After 5 minutes, turn left at the first fork that you come to. Less than a minute later, take a second left onto a narrower track. You are still following CAI 563. 2 minutes later take the right hand fork; you should see more CAI markers along this path.

2:23/1:13 After 5 minutes a path merges from the right and 2 minutes after this, turn right down a narrower path. The path is quite steep here so take care. Keep looking out for the red and white CAI signs. 3 minutes down the track you pass under an electricity line. The path twists down the hill and you pass under the power line two more times. Continue downhill and 7 minutes after the first passing the power line, you turn left at a Y shaped fork onto a grassy track.

2:40/1:30 3 minutes later you arrive at a house with a swimming pool. Turn left in front of the house and follow the track down. After 2 minutes, the road is surfaced with tarmac and you pass more houses on the left. A minute later, you come to a T-junction **(E)**. Here, you have the option of turning right for a quick detour to the Franciscan retreat of *Le Celle* (this is a 3 minute walk). To continue the walk, turn left.

2:46/1:36 This stretch of tarmac is not busy, but cars travel fairly quickly along it, so face the traffic unless on a left hand curve. Continue, ignoring tracks and driveways to either side. After 7 minutes, you pass a sign for the *Cappella Bentivoglio* next to a lay-by.

2:53/1:43 A further 3 minutes down the road, you pass the *Bentivoglio Chapel* on the left. After 8 minutes ignore a fairly large track going off to the right (this is the old road to *Cortona*). The tarmac road climbs and a minute later, you are at a T-junction on a sharp bend; turn left here **(F)**.

3:04/1:54 This is a short stretch of reasonably busy road, so keep on the grassy verge on the right. 2 minutes later, you come back to the *Hotel Corys* **(B)**. Turn right and ignore both the road to the left (next to a bar) and then a track going to the right. You are now retracing your steps back to the car. 2 minutes after the *Hotel Corys*, turn left onto the cypress lined track. After 13 minutes, you should be back at your car **(A)**.

Walking time: 3:21/2:11

2.3 The Rocca di Pierle (allow 3 hours 15 minutes)

Walking Time: 2 hours 28 minutes. Hard steep uphill climb, some rough terrain, sections can become overgrown in spring/summer, take secateurs.

The small village of *Pierle* is dominated by a ruined castle, which towers above the surrounding houses. The *Rocca di Pierle* was rebuilt in the 1360's but stands on the site of an earlier castle. The *Niccone Valley* has been a border area for thousands of years. At the eastern end of the valley, the border between the Etruscans and the Umbrian tribes followed the *River Tiber*. After the fall of the Roman Empire, the Byzantine corridor ran along the *Niccone Valley*. This strip of land allowed land communication between Byzantine controlled *Rome* and *Ravenna*. To the north and south of the corridor were lands under Lombard (Langobard) control. Fortifications were built in pairs along the corridor so that it could be defended from the hostile territory on either side.

In the medieval period, the border between the city-states of *Perugia* and *Cortona* ran along the valley and soldiers watched each other from their respective castles. During the Renaissance *Perugia* was absorbed into the Papal States and *Cortona* came under the control of the Florentines. The border between *Umbria* and *Tuscany* still runs along the *Niccone River* today. Look high above *Lisciano Niccone* and you will see the opposing castle.

The walk starts with a quick wander through the village and then climbs steeply to the ridge dividing the Tiber and Chiana-Arno water basins. The views at the top are fantastic; at the highest point (*Monte Ginezzo*) almost all of *Lake Trasimeno* is visible. After following the ridge it descends through thick wood and along an unpaved road back to *Pierle*. The climb can become overgrown in spring and summer, so wear trousers and take secateurs to cut back the vegetation.

If a hard climb is too much for you, you can still enjoy the walk along the ridge by parking at the top of the road pass between *Mercatale* and *Cortona*. You should see the red and white Club Alpini Italia (CAI) markers running north along the ridge. Follow them and you should pick up the route of the circular walk at point **(C)** after about 20 minutes. Obviously, if you do this, you have to return the way you came.

To Find The Start

The turning for *Pierle* is about 3km from *Mercatale* on the road running over the mountain between *Mercatale* and *Cortona*. It is marked with a brown and white sign for the *Rocca di Pierle*. Park on the right about 200m from the junction, there is just room to get a car off the

Rocca di Pierle

road. Look at the ridge behind you and you will see a dip between two rounded peaks. You should be standing there within an hour. If you can't park here, continue to the top of the village and park outside the church. However, you will miss the first 5 minutes of the walk through *Pierle*.

Walk Synopsis

(A) Walk through the village and continue up the unpaved road.

(B) Climb the rough track towards the ridge (you might need secateurs in late spring/summer).

(C) Follow the track along the ridge.

(D) Take the extension to the top of *Monte Ginezzo* **(E)**.

(E) Return to **(D)** and descend through the woods.

(F) Follow the unpaved road to **(B)** and then retrace your steps to **(A)**.

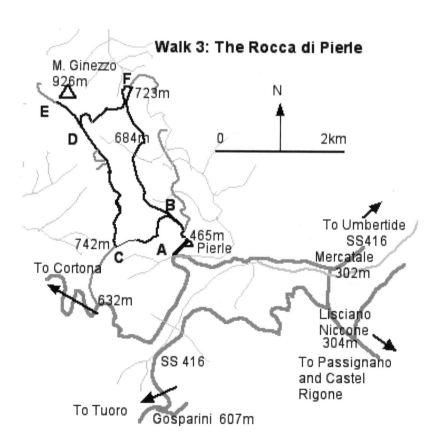

Walk 3: The Rocca di Pierle

M. Ginezzo 926m

F 723m

E

D 684m

684m

N

0 2km

B

465m Pierle

742m

C A

To Cortona

632m

To Umbertide
SS416
Mercatale
302m

Lisciano
Niccone
304m

To Passignano
and Castel
Rigone

SS 416

To Tuoro

Gosparini 607m

Start (A)

0:00   Set off up the tarmac road towards the village, after two minutes turn right and follow the road into *Pierle*. The turning is marked with red and white CAI signs. The narrow road winds up between old houses and the castle walls. The castle gate is locked but you can look through it into the keep. 5 minutes later you rejoin the road; turn right and continue upwards.

0:07   Stay on the main white road heading out of the village; ignore the turning on the right for *Borgo di Vagli*. 10 minutes after leaving the village you will see a steep track going up to the left. Look for the red and white CAI markers **(B)**.

0:17   Take this path up into the wood, it is steep and quite rough; at times you may have to use your secateurs. On the way up you should see more CAI markers. About 8 minutes after joining the track you will pass under an electricity line. 3 minutes later the main path dips in front of you and a minute later a track joins from the left.

0:29   Go straight on; you are now on the route of the Roman road between *Cortona* and *Pierle*. It remained the main road until the 19th Century. To the right you can see some ancient stone terracing and in places you walk on the old flagstones. After a few minutes you catch a glimpse of the ridge in front of you. 8 minutes after joining the old road, the track takes a sharp left. Continue climbing, and 5 minutes later you arrive at a T-junction where you take a right. After 4 minutes, the track bends sharply left and you emerge on the ridge straight away **(C)**.

0:46   Turn right onto the track running along the ridge, this is now marked with CAI markers for route 500. This path is part of the route taken by St Francis between *Lake Trasimeno* and *La Verna*, the Franciscan retreat in the mountains above *Arezzo*. Up here there are fantastic views of the *Niccone Valley* and the broad *Val di Chiana*.

0:46 Ahead, you should see some electricity poles, part of the same line you walked under earlier. The path along the ridge is obvious and well marked. After 10 minutes you might catch the first glimpse of the Lake behind you. 4 minutes later the track splits three ways. Take the track on the right (straight on), it climbs and after 4 minutes you pass a tall red and white antenna. The track descends and after 2 minutes you come to a junction; go straight on. After 5 minutes the path widens and splits in two around a triangle of vegetation. At this point, **(D)** it is well worth climbing up to *Monte Ginezzo*, an extension of 17 minutes. The ground has been badly churned by vehicles here. Before climbing up to the summit, stop and look for the path on the right that will take you down from the ridge. If you don't want to climb *Monte Ginezzo*, ignore the extension and take this path now.

1:11 **Extension to the ridge**

There are two paths to the summit: Divieto di Caccia signs on white poles mark the footpath to left; however, it is easier to take the right hand track that four-wheel drive vehicles use. 10 minutes later, you arrive at the summit **(E)**; an observation tower marks the spot. Almost all of *Lake Trasimeno* is visible and there are fantastic 360^0 views. Return the way you came, coming down is slightly quicker (7 minutes).
End of Extension

1:28 When you arrive back at the triangle of vegetation **(D)**, look for the path you found earlier (now on your left). The path descends into what is mainly an oak wood; ahead you can see a large white house. 10 minutes down the path you pass through a small clearing. 3 minutes further down you should get another glimpse of the house. Another 10 minutes and you pass a shrine to the Madonna (madonnina) on your left. Immediately after, you arrive at a T-junction **(F)**; turn right. You are now on the unpaved road returning to *Pierle*.

1:51   Continue down the gravel road, after 27 minutes, you pass the track that took you to the ridge. Keep going straight on and 7 minutes later you will be back in *Pierle*. Stay on the road rather than turning left into the village and 3 minutes later you will be back at your car **(A)**.

Walking time: 2:28

2.4   The Battle of Lake Trasimeno (allow over 2 hours)

Walking Time 1 hour 49 minutes. Relatively easy although some uphill.

The *Battle of Lake Trasimeno* took place on the northern shore of the Lake in 217 BC. It was one of the bloodiest battles (and worst defeats for the Romans) of the second Punic War. The Punic Wars were fought between the Mediterranean super-powers of *Rome* and *Carthage* (now in Tunisia); they ultimately led to the destruction of *Carthage* and the dominance of *Rome*.

The Carthaginian general at *Lake Trasimeno* was Hannibal. His unorthodox military tactics led to a series of defeats for the Romans. He came very close to halting the rise of their empire. The capture of *Rome* seemed a likely prospect after *Trasimeno*; if the non-Roman tribes had joined him in his campaign it could easily have happened. Memories of Hannibal's campaign were still fresh in the minds of the Romans when the Senate voted to completely destroy *Carthage* in the 3rd Punic War, 60 years later.

After crossing the Alps, and having won a resounding victory at *Trebbia* (near *Piacenza*), Hannibal's army was marching towards *Rome*. Hannibal was deliberately laying waste to the countryside and towns that he captured. This tactic was intended to provoke the Romans into a hasty, ill-considered attack. The Roman Commander, Caius Flaminius (Caio Flaminio), was advancing south down the *Val di Chiana* from *Arezzo*. He thought he was well behind the enemy army and was probably hoping to meet up with reinforcements south of *Perugia* before facing Hannibal in battle.

Hannibal had in fact deployed his army in the hills above *Sanguineto*, just to the north–west of *Tuoro*. From here he could watch and surprise the advancing Roman army. At dawn of 24 June 217 BC, the Romans were advancing into the ambush. During the night, Hannibal's men had lit fires on the hill near *Castel Rigone* to give the impression that they were still half a day's march away.

To the right of the marching Romans was the swampy shore of the Lake. The water level was higher than today, roughly equivalent to the route of the road between *Tuoro* and *Terontola*. To their left were the slopes hiding Hannibal's army. This carefully chosen topography meant that once the Roman army had entered the narrow gap between the *Lake* and hills, there was no escape. To make matters worse, fog blanketed the lake and lower ground, further obscuring the Carthiginians' presence from the Romans. Without warning, Hannibal attacked the marching Roman columns. They did not have time to organise into battle formation and, for the Romans; it rapidly became a case of every man for himself. 15,000 Romans were killed for the loss of 1,500 men in Hannibal's army.

It seems likely that several place names in the area have origins resulting from the Battle. *Sanguineto*, (the place of blood), *Ossaia* (the place of bones), *Sepoltaglia*, (the place of tombs), *Malpasso* (bad pass) and *Pian di Marte* (Plain of Mars, the Roman God of War). Others claim that Marte is a corruption of martire, Italian for martyr, and refers to the Roman prisoners who were executed there (see walk).

For the next two years, the Romans avoided meeting Hannibal in open battle. When they tried again at *Cannae* in southern Italy (215 BC), they lost 70,000 men out of an army of 80,000 deployed against a force of around 45,000 on Hannibal's side. In a battle still studied by military tacticians, Hannibal deployed his heavy Gaulish infantry in a thin convex curve. As the Roman infantry attacked, the curve gradually fell back into a concave shape. Hannibal had held his elite African troops in reserve and they now attacked the Roman flanks. The Romans found themselves surrounded on three sides. Meanwhile, the superior Carthaginian cavalry chased the Roman cavalry from the battlefield and then attacked the infantry from behind. Again, Hannibal failed to take *Rome* after the battle and gradually the Romans learnt to copy his tactics. He was defeated in Africa 13 years later (202 BC) by the Roman general Scipio who had been one of the few to escape from *Cannae*. Instead of fulfilling his dream of destroying *Rome*, Hannibal had inadvertenly taught them the military tactics that helped them to create their empire.

To Find The Start

The walk starts in the hamlet of *Sanguineto*, which is located off the old road running between *Tuoro* and *Terontola di Cortona*. For those who wish to buy some quality local produce, there are plenty of farm shops selling olive oil along this route. The main area of fighting took place in the plain below the hamlet. Driving to the start of the walk, you pass several interpretation points with information about the Battle.

The turning for *Sanguineto* is on the right if you are coming from *Tuoro*. As you drive along, look out for *Sosta no.9* on the left (interpretation point no.9 on the Battle Trail), there is a farm shop on the right (signed *Vendita Diretta Frutta Verdure Piantine*) and a few hundred metres further on you will find the track for *Sanguineto*. It is marked by two umbrella pines and comes up suddenly as you drive around a bend.

If you are coming from the direction of *Cortona* and *Terontola* look out on the right for *Sosta no.2* (interpretation point no.2 on the Battle Trail). The umbrella pines marking the *Sanguineto* turning are just ahead to the left. Drive into the hamlet and follow the signs for *Agriturismo Il Giardino*. Drive past the Agriturismo and park on the left just as the tarmac road turns into an unpaved track heading uphill. Be careful not to block a small track going down into the olive grove.

Walk Synopsis

(A) Climb the track from *Sanguineto* up to the ridge high above the Lake.

(B) Follow the track along the ridge in an easterly direction.

(C) Take the track down from the ridge; this becomes a tarmac road at the bottom.

(D) Turn right and follow the road back to *Sanguineto* **(A)**.

Walk 4. The Battle of Lake Trasimeno

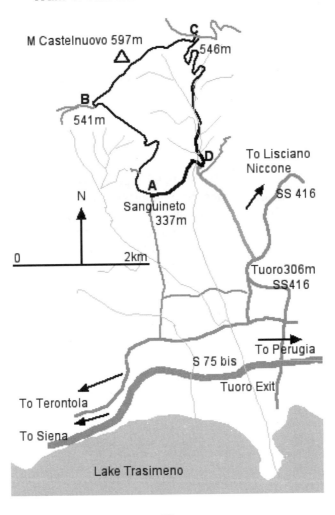

Start (A)

0:00 Take the track going up the hill. (To the right is a tarmac drive with a private sign). After four minutes you should notice the first red and white Club Alpini Italia (CAI) marker painted on a rock. At a fork a minute later, take the main track going to the right; it is clearly marked by CAI.

0:05 Stay on the main track until you reach the ridge; ignore all tracks leading off to the left and right. The CAI markers are less frequent along this stretch. 15 minutes later, the gradient starts to level out. 7 minutes later, you arrive at the ridge. The ridge track is clearly marked by the CAI in both directions, ignore the two rougher tracks on the left and follow the better-made track around to the right **(B)**.

0:27 After a few minutes, *Cortona* should be visible to the northwest (slightly back to the left). Keep following the main track; again clearly marked by the CAI. 22 minutes after joining the ridge, a dip in the ridge enables you to see the track for a fair distance in front before it disappears into a wood. 3 minutes later, you should be at the bottom of the dip, a track joins from the left and immediately after a well maintained track leads down to the right **(C)**.

0:52 Take the right hand track (towards the Lake) and follow it as it winds its way down the hill. 29 minutes from the ridge you pass a one storey stone building with fence and olive grove. The descent starts to level out at this point.

1:21 5 minutes after the building, the track forks, take the right track (to the left is a sign which reads *Località Nuvola*). The track follows a stream on the right. 5 minutes later on, ignore a minor road to the left and the track turns into a tarmac road. You pass some new houses and 3 minutes after the tarmac starts, you take the road to the right **(D)**, this is sign-posted *Sanguineto* and *Agriturismo Il Giardino*.

1.34 7 minutes later you pass interpretation point no.6 on the left, 5 minutes later you are at a fork in the middle of *Sanguineto*. Turn right towards the *Agriturismo Il Giardino* and 3 minutes later you should be at your car **(A)**.

1.49   If you have been stopping at the interpretation points, you may wish to visit *Sosta no.7,* which is not on the walk. Return in your car along the tarmac road past *Sosta no.6.* If you turn right at the end of the road you will pass a sign for *no. 7.* The sign is pointing right down a track towards a house. (To find it you have to walk through the olive groves, turn left when you arrive at the road below and walk along the road for another 200 metres). *Sosta no.7* is thought to be the pits (ustrini) where the bodies from the battle were burnt. It is thought that Hannibal ordered that the burning to stop the spread of disease (a kind of charm offensive towards the locals). If you return to your car and continue along the road you will arrive in the centre of *Tuoro.*

Walking time: 1:49

2.5 Above Lisciano Niccone
(allow 2 hours 45 minutes)

Walking time: 2 hours 9 minutes. Relatively easy, although some rough terrain.

This walk is on the paths high above *Lisciano Niccone*; these have been sign posted as *Percorso Trekking* (trekking routes) by the Comune (local council). It largely follows contours and ridges, so there is less climbing and descending than in most of the other walks. Having said this, do not expect it to be completely level! Again, there are great views of *Lake Trasimeno*.

To Find The Start

Take the turning sign-posted *Percorso Trekking* on the road between *Lisciano Niccone* and *Castel Rigone*. This is at the highest point between the 8 and 9km markers and is on the right if you are coming from *Lisciano Niccone* and on the left if you are coming from *Castel Rigone* or *Passignano*.

Follow the track for about 1.5km until the road forks. Take the right turn; again sign-posted *Percorso Trekking*. Drive past a modern house on the left and park shortly afterwards at the next fork. (the track straight ahead climbs fairly steeply) Up here, there is a fantastic view of *Lake Trasimeno*.

Note: if you are coming from *Tuoro*, there is an alternative starting point **(E)**. This adds a total of 16 minutes to the walking time but will save you a lot of time in the car. At the top of the pass (SS 416) between *Tuoro* and *Lisciano Niccone* there is a road on the right next to the bar/restaurant called *Lo Scoiattolo*. Drive along this road for approximately 2km, past houses built in a strange mixture of architectural styles. Park at a junction where the main track curves sharply left; there is a sign for *Monte Castiglione*. Other distinguishing features are the dense pine hedge on the left (screening the garden to a house) and a house on the right; this has a stone garden wall with a metal fence on top. Take the track going straight on; to your right on a tree you should see a red and white Club Alpini Italia (CAI) marker and green and yellow MTB (mountain bike) sign. Follow the track into the wood and when you arrive at the first junction 8 minutes later, take the left and you join the main walk at **(D)**.

Walk Synopsis

(A) Descend past *San Bartolomeo* and enter woods, eventually the track emerges onto a wider unpaved road.

(B) Turn right and follow the unpaved road, great views of *Lake Trasimeno.*

(C) Cross the open ground and then the path becomes enclosed by woods.

(D) Turn right, after a while the path emerges from the woods and you are treated to more views before arriving back at the car **(A)**.

If you use the alternative starting point **(E)**, you join the walk at **(D)**.

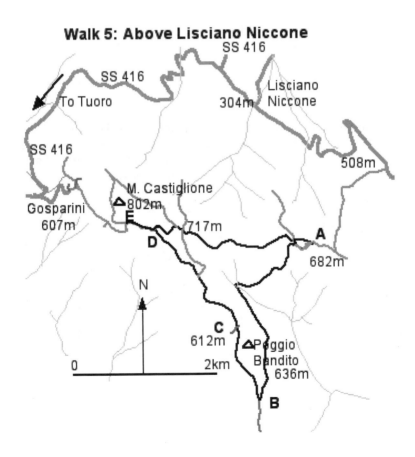

Walk 5: Above Lisciano Niccone

Start (A)

0:00   Take the track that climbs steeply in front of you. You will recognise this route if you have done the *Pian di Marte* walk. After 4 minutes you come to a crossroads; there are three tracks to choose from, take the left (ahead is sign posted *Tracciato 1+2* and *Monte Castiglione* and the track to the right is sign posted *Tracciato 2+3*).

0:04   After a minute ignore a track joining from the left. Continue for another 5 minutes and you come to the church of *San Bartolomeo*, which has been restored as a house. The Lake disappears behind the ridge in front of you at this point. **Note:** in the near future the road will be diverted around *San Bartolomeo*, this should not overly affect the walk, but you won't go right past the house.

0:10   Follow the track around to the right and pass the house on your left, the track forks just after; take the rougher track going straight on. In winter, this track can become quite muddy. 4 minutes beyond *San Bartolomeo*, you pass first a ruin on the left and then another on the right. Another 2 minutes and the track forks again. Ignore the fainter right hand track and continue straight on.

0:16   Keep on the main track for another 29 minutes and the track emerges onto a wider, gravelled road opposite a pinewood. Turn right and start to climb up the track **(B)**.

0:45   The track is sign-posted with red and white no.3 and no.50 markers by CAI and green and yellow MTB signs. There are wonderful views of the lake to the left, after 12 minutes, you pass a sign which reads *Punto Panoramico*. This appears to state the obvious, but on closer inspection, it seems to be pointing up to the summit of *Poggio Bandito* (635m).

0:57   Another 4 minutes along the track, you arrive at a fork in the track. Go straight on and pass a farmhouse on the right **(C)**. The dogs will run up and down barking on the other side of the fence. After 4 minutes the fence on the right hand side ends. If you look back to the right at this point, you can see *San Bartolomeo*, the restored church that you passed earlier.

1:05   As you leave the fenced area behind, the track crosses an open space and 10 minutes later it becomes enclosed by oak and broom scrub. MTB and CAI signs continue to mark the way. After 5 minutes, the track forks; continue straight on. The path markers are scarcer along this stretch.

1:20   After 7 minutes the wood opens out and there is a house with a great view of the Lake on your left. 2 minutes later, you pass the drive to the house. A further 3 minutes along the track, you pass another (empty) house up on your right. Continue for 4 minutes and you come to a junction; turn right here **(D)**.

Note: If you used the alternative starting point, turn left and you will arrive back at the car **(E)** in 8 minutes.

1:36   After 3 minutes you come to a fork, continue straight on (left is sign-posted *Monte Castiglione*). Just after, the track splits three ways next to a madonnina. Take the middle track going straight on. Continue for 11 minutes and the track emerges from the woods and dips towards a saddle on the ridge.

1:50   2 minutes later, you pass a minor track on the left, the track you are on climbs up to the other side of the saddle and 7 minutes later you pass the track to a concrete building on the right. You can make a small detour here and climb up to the terrace on the roof to enjoy the 360^0 panoramic view with a telescope provided by the comune of *Lisciano Niccone*.

1:59   Continue along the main track and 4 minutes later it curves sharply right next to a ruin on your left. After 2 minutes, you come to the crossroads near the start of the walk. Continue straight on (the track to the left is sign-posted *Traccito 2+3* and the track you have just come along is sign-posted *Traccito 1+2* and *Monte Castiglione*). After 4 minutes retracing your steps, you arrive back at the car **(A)**.

Walking time: 2:09

Note: If you are using the alternative starting point, turn right at the crossroads, you are now on the descent to *San Bartolomeo* described in the first paragraph.

2.6 The Pian di Marte (allow 4 hours 30 minutes)

3 hours 31 minutes walking time. Some steep sections.

This walk starts in the *Pian di Marte* (the *Plain of Mars*). Mars was the Roman god of war and the name might relate to the *Battle of Lake Trasimeno* in 217 BC. Six thousand Roman soldiers forced their way out of the trap that Hannibal had set for them on the north shore of the Lake. They made their way over the ridge to the *Pian di Marte* where they were persuaded to surrender. Roman reports tell us that those of Roman origin were then killed and the others released so that they could take news of the defeat to *Perugia* and on to *Rome*.

Torre di Fiume

The *Pian di Marte* is a valley overlooked by a medieval tower, the *Torre di Fiume*. The tower is all that remains of a larger castle. It formed part of a chain of defences at the northern end of Perugia's territory. Records show that the tower dates back to 1313, when it was rebuilt on the site of an earlier fortification.

The idea of moving here began to germinate in our minds when my wife Emma, oblivious to our lack of finances, suggested that we buy the tower and restore it. Less than a year later we were living here as the proud owners of a ruined farmhouse and with a second daughter on the way.

During this walk you will come across cows. If they make you nervous, carry a walking stick and move steadily along the path towards the cows, waving your stick. They will soon move out of your way. If you have a dog and the cows become agitated by its presence, the accepted advice is to let it off the lead; it can easily avoid the cows but you can't. Look out for the famous white Chianina cattle, descendants of the cattle used by the Etruscans and Romans for sacrifices.

To Find The Start

The main road through the *Pian di Marte* runs between *Lisciano Niccone* and *Castel Rigone*. Take the road marked with a brown sign for the Agriturismo *Villa La Stampa*. It is on the valley floor betwwen the 4 and 5km markers. It is on your right if you are coming from *Lisciano Niccone* and on your left if you are approaching from *Castel Rigone* or *Passignano*. Park about 100 metres along the road on the left; there is enough space to get the car off the road. On your right is a strange prefabricated church and to your left you can see the *Torre di Fiume*.

Walk Synopsis

(A) Walk towards *Villa Stampa*, then turn left; in front you can see the *Torre di Fiume*.

(B) Pass through the farm, the route then begins a long climb.

(C) Continue climbing past a modern house on a ridge.

(D) Descend past *San Bartolomeo* and enter the woods.

(E) Emerge onto a wide unpaved road, there are great views along this stretch.

(F) Descend from the ridge into the woods.

(G) Take the path to the *Torre di Fiume*.

(H) Continue the descent until you arrive at the valley floor near a restored house.

(I) Follow the track through the fields and turn left onto the tarmac road taking you back to the start **(A)**.

Walk 6: Pian di Marte

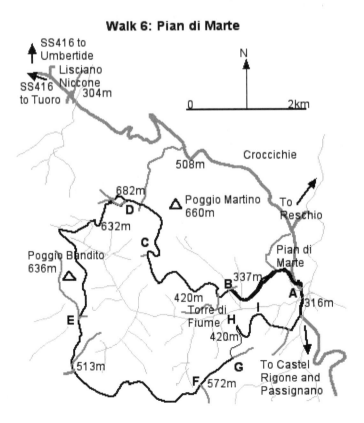

Start (A)

0:00   Walk along the road towards *Villa La Stampa*, the large yellow building on the hill in front of you. After 4 minutes, take the left turn at a fork (straight on is signed for *Villa La Stampa*). 4 minutes later, you pass an irrigation reservoir on the left and a minute after this, the drive to a house on the left. 4 minutes further and you pass a converted water mill on your left. The track curves to the right and 2 minutes later, you pass a tobacco-drying tower on your left and enter a farmyard. Follow the road through the farm and take the left fork immediately after the buildings; the tarmac ends here **(B)**.

0:15   Tobacco drying towers are a common feature of the landscape. Stone farmhouses often have them incorporated in their structure. Later versions usually stand apart from other buildings and are constructed with blocks. Towers are no longer used to dry tobacco; it now takes place in ugly industrial sheds, a less romantic but more efficient process. Tobacco growing will probably disappear from the area as subsidies are being phased out by 2014.

   3 minutes after passing the tobacco tower, a makeshift gate may block the track. If it is shut when you approach, close it after you. At this point in the walk, you will come across cows. If they are blocking the track, walk steadily towards them (waving your stick if you have one) and they will move out of the way.

0:18   A minute later, you pass a large open sided shed on your right and a ruined house is visible directly in front. Another minute and you pass the ruin in the field on your left. The track forks; turn right and head uphill.

0:20   10 minutes later, you pass a house undergoing a complete rebuild (Feb 2005), on your left. 3 minutes beyond this, you pass a watering hole on the right; there are usually a few cows here. 13 minutes after the watering hole, you arrive at another makeshift gate, be sure to close it behind you. 4 minutes beyond the gate you come to a junction **(C)**, turn right (uphill). By now, the lake should be visible to the south.

0:50 7 minutes later a minor track joins from the left, keep going straight on. 6 minutes after this, you come to a fork; go left, passing an agricultural shed. 3 minutes later, you arrive at a junction with three options.

1:06 Take the middle track signed *Monte Castiglione Percorso Trekking* which heads towards a fairly unattractive house ahead on the ridge (the track to the left goes through a gate into a field). 3 minutes later, you pass the house on your left. 4 minutes beyond the house there is a fork, take the track that climbs steeply in front of you. You will recognise this route if you have done the *Above Lisciano Niccone* walk.

1:13 After another 4 minutes you come to a crossroads **(D)**; there are three tracks to choose from, take the left (ahead is sign posted *Tracciato 1+2* and *Monte Castiglione* and the track to the right is sign posted *Tracciato 2+3*). After a minute ignore a track joining from the left. Continue for another 5 minutes and you come to the church of *San Bartolomeo*, which has been restored as a house. The Lake disappears behind the ridge in front of you at this point. **Note:** in the near future the road will be diverted around *San Bartolomeo*, this should not affect the walk

1:23 Follow the road around to the right, passing the converted church on your left. There is a fork in the track just beyond the house. Leave the well-maintained track curving to the left and take the rougher track straight ahead. 2 minutes beyond the restored house, you pass a ruin on the left and then another a minute later on your right. After another 2 minutes, there is another fork, ignore the fainter track to the right and continue straight on.

1:28 3 minutes later, the track turns sharply left. 10 minutes later there are minor tracks to the left and right; keep to the middle track. 12 minutes further and you arrive at a junction with a pine plantation on the other side of the road **(E)**.

1:53 Turn left onto the well-made track. Ignore a drive immediately to your left with a *Strada Privata* sign. The track is flanked by pine trees on the right and is clearly signed by the Club Alpini Italia

(CAI) with red and white markers for the whole of this stretch. You can also look out for diamond shaped MTB (mountain bike) markers in green and yellow. 5 minutes along the track, the lake comes into view ahead of you (south). The view here is incredible. After another 5 minutes, go straight over a crossroads. (To the right is a tarmac road down to *Passignano*, to the left is a minor track and a madonnina).

2:03   3 minutes after the crossroads, you come to a fork; follow the main track to the left. 3 minutes further on, you pass a house on the right, ignore the drive and continue straight on. Just after the house, the track forks, take the left. After 3 minutes, you pass a hide on the right.

2:12   A minute later, a large house becomes visible on the ridge ahead. Follow the main track towards this house. Ignore any minor paths or tracks and 17 minutes later you pass the drive to the house on your right. 6 minutes later, there is a track going down to the left, continue straight on and 50 metres after this you come to a second track on the left. The junction is sign-posted by both CAI and MTB markers. Turn left onto this track **(F)**.

2:36   The track descends through oak woods down to the *Pian di Marte*. After 3 minutes stay on the main track and ignore a fainter track in front to the left. 2 minutes later ignore another track to your left. Continue for another 6 minutes and there is a junction; take the track which goes straight on. Take care; the track is deeply rutted and very steep (if the descent is too steep you can turn right here and follow the gentler gradient until you rejoin the route at the next junction, in this case you will be on the track which joins from the right).

2:47   After another 2 minutes' descent a track joins from the right, continue straight on. 3 minutes further down, the wood opens out into scrub vegetation. Look for a single oak tree on your right and a narrow path to your left, (there is a tiny red arrow painted onto this tree pointing back up the path) **(G)**.

2:52   Turn left here onto the path, shortly after joining the path, it curves to the left and descends through oak woods. After 3 minutes, there is a CAI marker on a tree on the left. A further 2 minutes on and the *Torre di Fiume* is visible directly ahead. You pass through abandoned olive groves; these trees must have supplied the inhabitants of the tower and the associated settlement with oil. 2 minutes later you should be standing near the tower **(H)**.

2:59   Continuing the walk, go on down the path, there is a large ruined house and an old stone built wall on your left. After 2 minutes, you come to a junction; turn right, heading down. 8 minutes further on you pass a ruined house and church on the right.

3:09   2 minutes later the track curves left in front of the fence of a newly restored house **(I)**. Follow the track around the fence and 5 minutes later, you pass the drive to the house on your right. Continue straight on, skirting around the edge of the fields.

3:16   2 minutes later there is another fork; follow the main track around to the left. 4 minutes further on you arrive at a T-junction with the tarmac road running along the valley floor; turn left here. After 3 minutes you cross a bridge; ignore the tracks to both sides. 3 minutes later you pass a house on the right and a minute after that you arrive at the turning for *Villa La Stampa* on your left. Turn here and 2 minutes later you are back at your car **(A)**.

Walking time: 3:31

2.7   From Passignano To Terontola
(allow 7- 8 hours with break)

Walking time: 5 hours 24 minutes. A steep climb, some rough sections.

This is not a circular walk, but it does have the advantage that the route is from *Passignano* railway station to the station at *Terontola di Cortona*. I have described the walk in this direction so that the sun will be behind you for the majority of the trip if you start early in the morning. The route links sections from the *Pian di Marte*, *Above Lisciano Niccone,* and the *Battle of Lake Trasimeno* walks. It is mainly along ridges with superb views of *Lake Trasimeno.*

To Find The Start

Both towns have exits on the 75 bis, the dual carriageway which runs along the north shore of the Lake. Both railway stations are fairly easy to find but I would consider parking at *Terontola* and catching a train to *Passignano* at the start of the walk, you won't feel like waiting for a train at the end of it! I couldn't wait 40 minutes and took a taxi with my friend Tom (15 Euros).

Another good reason to catch the train from *Terontola* is that parking is easier. The car park at *Passignano* station is small and most of the town car parks charge by the hour (or 5.20 Euros for the whole day). The *Terontola* station car park is located on the other side of the railway line; follow the rather small signposts on the SS 71 which lead you under the tracks and back round to the station. In the event of the station car park being full, find a side street within *Terontola* and make your way to the station on foot.

Train times change annually, so check the day before you walk. The Italian Railway's website is **www.trenitalia.it** . There is the opportunity to stop along the route and have lunch at *Lo Scoiattolo*, the bar/restaurant at the top of the pass between *Lisciano Niccone* and *Tuoro*. If you plan to do this, avoid Tuesdays when it is closed. Another option is the restaurant nearby at the *Hotel La Cima*, but I can't tell you anything about it as I've never eaten there.

Walk Synopsis

(A) Leave *Passignano* station and walk towards the town, climb up to the ridge high above the Lake.

(B) Walk along the ridge track, this section is part of the *Pian di Marte* walk in reverse.

(C) Keep following the track, eventually you pass a farmhouse with barking dogs,

(D) Cross an open space and then the track becomes enclosed by woods.

(E) Emerge from the woods and follow the road past houses down to *Gosparini*.

(F) Cross the SS 416; the track climbs once more. Take the path along the ridge and enter a wood near a stone marker. Continue through the wood arriving at a junction near cypress trees.

(G) Continue through the wood and then descend down a steep, badly rutted track.

(H) The view opens out, continue along the ridge until you arrive at the track down to *Terontola*.

(I) Descend, go through the village of *Cortoreggio* and arrive at the road between *Terontola* and *Tuoro*.

(J) Cross the road and enter *Terontola*, finally arriving at the station **(K)**.

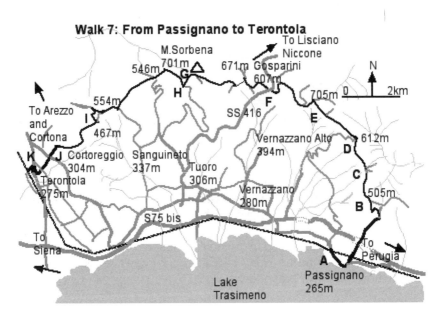

Walk 7: From Passignano to Terontola

- 44 -

Start (A)

0:00   Turn right as you walk out of *Passignano* station and walk towards the town centre. After 2 minutes you cross the railway. 2 minutes beyond this, you will see a large building on your left called the *Municipio* (the town hall), and a church in front. On your right is a building with a sign reading *Gelateria Artigianale*, (home made ice cream), and behind that, *Lake Trasimeno*.

0:04   Cross the road here and head along *Via Venanzio Gabriotti*. You pass the bar *Tre Torri* (the last chance to buy water) and the road opens out into a car park. Cross the car park and 2 minutes after turning onto *Via Venanzio Gabriotti*, you arrive at some steps sign posted with the distinctive red and white markers of the Club Alpini Italia (CAI).

0:06   Go up the steps (there are two sets) and turn right at the top. Almost immediately, turn left onto *Via Dell'Asilo* (the road going straight on leads through an arch into the old town). Shortly after, turn right onto *Via Don Nazzareno Tabarrini*. It is 2 minutes since you were at the bottom of the steps. Continue for 5 minutes and you come to a crossroads; go straight over onto *Via San Crispolto*.

0:13   This is the longest climb in the walk; you are heading for the ridge high above the Lake. After 9 minutes you pass some mobile phone masts, one has been badly disguised as a tree with green netting. The road continues upwards, passing houses (and barking dogs) on both sides.

0:22   12 minutes later you pass a modern villa on your right and just after it, you come to a junction. The tarmac road continues steeply upwards, leave it and take the track on your left marked path no.50 by the CAI. This path follows a much gentler gradient and 14 minutes later joins the ridge next to a conifer plantation **(B)**.

0:48   Turn left onto the track running along the ridge, after 4 minutes you come to a junction next to a shrine. The track splits four ways here, take the second track from the left, this passes to the left of the shrine and is marked with a leaping deer sign as well as CAI and MTB markers.

0:52   The track heads towards an empty house and passes in front of it. If you have done the *Pian di Marte* walk, you will recognise this stretch. Continue, and 14 minutes later, you come to a junction, follow the main track straight on and ignore the two smaller tracks on your right **(C)**. The next section will be familiar if you have completed the *Above Lisciano Niccone* walk.

1:06   The track is sign-posted with red and white no.3 and no.50 markers by CAI and green and yellow MTB (mountain bike) signs. There are wonderful views of the lake to the left, after 12 minutes, you pass a sign which reads *Punto Panoramico*. This appears to state the obvious, but on closer inspection, it seems to be pointing up to the summit of *Poggio Bandito* (635m).

1:18   Another 4 minutes along the track, you arrive at a fork. Go straight on and pass a farmhouse on the right **(D)**. The dogs will run up and down barking on the other side of the fence. After 4 minutes, the fence on the right hand side ends.

1:26   Leaving the fenced area behind, the track crosses an open space and 10 minutes later, enters oak and broom scrub. MTB and CAI signs continue to mark the way. After 5 minutes, the track forks; continue straight on. Ignore the more obviously marked path going up to your right.

1:41   The path markers are scarcer along this stretch, after 7 minutes the wood opens out and there is a house with a great view of the lake on your left. 2 minutes later, you pass the drive to the house. A further 3 minutes along the track, you pass another (empty) house up on your right. Continue for 4 minutes and you come to a junction, turn left here **(E)**.

1:57   After 7 minutes you come to a junction, continue straight on, (to the right, it is sign posted *Monte Castiglione*).

2:04   This part of the walk passes through a suburb of holiday houses with great lake views. Those that are occupied have the standard barking dog. After 4 minutes, ignore a track going off down to the left. After another 9 minutes, ignore a CAI marked path heading up to the right. Continue for a further 10 minutes and you arrive at *Lo Scoiattolo*, the restaurant/bar at *Gosparini* **(F)**. This is the hamlet at top of the pass between *Tuoro* and *Lisciano Niccone* on the SS 416.

2:27   Feeling refreshed, head out of the restaurant and across the SS 416. Take the track directly opposite; it is sign posted as path no.50 by the CAI. On your left is a house with a fence. After 6 minutes a path joins from the left marked CAI nos.3 and 50, continue straight on. A further 7 minutes and you come to a junction, turn right, you are still heading up.

2:40   After 3 minutes you reach the ridge; pay attention here. Just before the main track forks, take the fainter path to the left between some fence posts. This path runs through the pasture and follows the line of the ridge, the Tuscany-Umbria border. This route has CAI markers but you could easily miss it. The views on this stretch of the walk are fantastic: you have the Lake on your left, *Cortona* and mountains to your right.

2:43   After 6 minutes there is a crossroads of paths, continue straight on towards the woods ahead. After another 2 minutes, the track splits next to a stone marker. Continue straight up into the woods. 5 minutes later, you come to a crossroads, turn right and follow the CAI markers. 12 minutes later, you come to a junction with cypress trees growing in the middle **(G)**. Turn right and follow the CAI 565 markers.

3:08   After 11 minutes, the track curves sharply right next to a *Pericolo Incendio* sign. 2 minutes later you come to a junction, take the track to the left, it heads steeply downwards for the next 10 minutes. There are plenty of CAI markers to confirm that you are on the right path. The track is badly eroded and this is the roughest part of the entire walk, so take care. At the bottom, you come to a T-junction; turn right **(H)**.

3:31 After 5 minutes, you pass a couple of minor tracks on your right. There is another track on the left 2 minutes later. A further 12 minutes along the track you come to a saddle with tracks leading off to the left and right. Continue straight on, this section is shared with the *Battle of Lake Trasimeno* walk.

3:50 After 20 minutes, you pass a minor track on the left; there is a CAI marker and an MTB sign on a tree to the right. 8 minutes later, you come to a junction where the main track curves left, turn right (there are two tracks on the right but they join up shortly after). You have now left the section shared with the *Battle of Lake Trasimeno* walk. After 6 minutes, you come to another junction, take the right, which continues along the ridge and is still signed CAI no.565. A further 8 minutes along and you come to a junction **(I)**. Ahead to your right is the drive to a house; straight on the ridge path continues; and sharply back to your left is a track leading down from the ridge. Take this track; you are now on the descent to *Terontola Station*.

4:32 After 7 minutes, you pass the drive to a house on the right. Another 3 minutes and you come to a junction with four options, take the descending track furthest to the right. Continue down on this track, ignore tracks and drives to houses, which become more frequent the further you go.

4:42 17 minutes from the junction, a tarmac drive curves left in front of a house; follow the unpaved track passing to the right of the house. The track goes between fenced in olive groves and holiday apartments.

4:59   3 minutes later it becomes a paved road and passes through the village of *Cortoreggio*. 10 minutes after the tarmac starts, you come to a crossroads with the road between *Terontola* and *Tuoro* **(J)**. Go straight over (sign posted *Stazione*).

5:12   The road leads into the centre of *Terontola*, after 6 minutes, go straight over a crossroads and 2 minutes later you arrive at the main road through *Terontola*, the SS 71. Turn right here and 2 minutes later cross the road and turn left to the station. After 2 minutes you arrive there **(K)**.

Walking time: 5:24

2.8 The Leaning Tower of Vernazzano
(allow 2 hours 30 minutes)

Walking Time 2 hours 4 minutes. Relatively easy.

This walk has lovely views across *Lake Trasimeno* and has the extra attraction of the *Leaning Tower of Vernazzano*. The tower and a ruined chapel are the remnants of a once thriving fortress and village. The castle lost its importance as the constant warfare of the medieval and the Renaissance periods came to an end.

In addition, the use of cannon meant that stone fortifications became obsolete. The main road between *Cortona* and *Perugia* was moved nearer to the lake and the castle left high on the hillside. Erosion in the steep gullies on two sides of the castle caused several landslides and on the 2 April 1753, an earthquake left the tower leaning at its alarming angle. In 2004, cables were attached to the tower and fixed at the other end to a reinforced concrete block buried in in the ground. When you see the tower, you will be amazed that it stood unaided for 251 years.

An additional point of historical interest relates to the *Battle of Lake Trasimeno* in 217BC. The vanguard of the Roman army, comprising 6000 men, is thought to have broken through Hannibal's light infantry on the slopes covered by this walk. They made their way to the *Pian di Marte* (see walk), where they surrendered.

To Find The Start

Park your car at the top of *Tuoro sul Trasimeno*. Coming from *Umbertide* on the SS 416, you will find the car park on the left after passing the town sign (about 300 - 400m).

If you are coming from the lake, take the SS 416 straight through *Tuoro* towards *Lisciano Niccone* and *Umbertide* (take the *Tuoro sul Trasimeno* exit from the 75 bis). You pass a newspaper kiosk on your left and then the public gardens on your right. A little further and the road bends to the right; the car park is just after this on the right.

Walk Synopsis

(A)   Go through the public gardens and head out of the town on *Via Pozzo*.
(B)   The track takes you past an olive grove on your left and a wood on your right.

(C) Climb along the cypress-lined track, it levels out and then climbs again arriving at a junction.

(D) The track levels out once more, then climbs through sheep pasture, arriving at a farmhouse.

(E) Leaving the farmhouse, the track passes through woods and olive groves and curves around two restored houses. Take the track which heads towards the leaning tower; you may catch a glimpse of it as you pass between more vineyards, olive trees and woods.

(F) From the tower, descend into the ravine, cross the bridge and you arrive at a tarmac road in *Vernazzano*.

(G) Follow the road down to the village of *Vernazzano Basso*.

(H) Take the unpaved road back towards *Tuoro*, after a while the road becomes paved. Retrace your steps to **(A)**, stopping for refreshments in the town square should you feel the need!

Walk 8: The Leaning Tower of Vernazzano

Start (A)

0:00   Walk down towards the town from the car park and you arrive at the public gardens in a couple of minutes. Walk through the gardens, and at the far left of the gardens you will find the *Tourist Information Office* (*Pro Loco*). Take a left onto *Via Ritorta* and follow the road down. After 2 minutes, turn left onto *Via Pozzo*, the sign has been missing for the last year so if there is no sign you are probably on the right road!

0:04   Head straight down this road, ignoring *Via G. Mazzini* on the right and then a left going up to some houses. 4 minutes later you might notice a red and white CAI (Club Alpini Italia) marker on a tree (no.2), the road then curves to the right and then to the left. Directly after the bend continue straight on at a fork marked by cypress trees. Keep going straight down and 2 minutes later you cross a small bridge; turn right at the junction just after **(B)**.

0:10 One minute later you cross a second bridge, there are olive groves on your left and a wood on your right. 4 minutes after the second bridge, the track forks, take the less obvious left track (blocked to vehicles with a mound of earth). Almost immediately turn left again **(C)** onto a cypress-lined track and head uphill. Someone seems to spend a lot of time using earth-moving machinery here, so you may have to cross a ditch to reach the track.

0:15 After 4 minutes the track levels out. 3 minutes later a house becomes visible straight ahead. A minute later the track bends sharply to the right in front of the house and climbs once more. 2 minutes after this you arrive at a fork. Turn left along a rutted track (ignoring a second track which goes off to the left immediately afterwards) **(D)**. You may encounter temporary sheep gates along the way; if you do, please make sure you shut them behind you.

0:25 3 minutes along the track, you pass an open sided agricultural building on your right. 2 minutes later you pass between a row of fence posts; look for a CAI marker. The path bends to the left and follows the electricity line up the hill. There is a great view of the lake to the right. Continue up the path and after 5 minutes there is a house on your right **(E)**.

0:35 At the junction immediately afterwards, leave the line of electricity poles and turn right (sometimes there is a temporary gate here). You pass the house on the right. There are sheep here so keep dogs on a lead. Dogs may bark at you from behind the fence. Follow the track and after 7 minutes you pass two restored farmhouses on the right. The road curves around these houses and a minute later, you find yourself at a fork.

0:43 Take the left turn, after 3 minutes you catch a glimpse of the leaning tower ahead to the right. Another 3 minutes and you pass a CAI marker on a tree on your right, the road then enters a wood. In winter, you can just see the tower through the trees to the right. You are walking along the bank of a steep ravine. On the left you pass the entrance to a campsite. 9 minutes after entering the wood the road crosses the stream and doubles back along the other bank.

0:58   One minute later the tower appears in front of you. Turn right onto the track running alongside the fence and head straight towards the tower. A CAI sign marks the way. 3 minutes later you arrive at the tower **(F)**.

1:02   Standing in front of the tower so that it is leaning to your left, look for a CAI marked path which descends steeply into a ravine. At the bottom, the path turns right and follows the stream. Shortly after, cross the stream on a wooden bridge. Follow the path and 8 minutes after leaving the tower, you arrive at a tarmac road in *Vernazzano* **(G)**.

1:10   Turn right onto the road. Walk downhill, after a while the road levels and you pass 2 houses on the right hand side. 15 minutes after starting on the tarmac you reach the village of *Vernazzano Basso*. Turn right near a large iron cross, just after passing a small public space on your right **(H)**.

1:25   Cross the small bridge and turn left immediately afterwards (to the right is a signpost for *Agrituristica Casa Colonica*). The tarmac finishes straight away and the track continues through olive groves and fields. 13 minutes after crossing the bridge ignore *Via Castelonchio* to the right.

1:38   Shortly after this, ignore the road to the left and continue straight along *Via Casa Piano*. 7 minutes later the road curves sharply left in *Cerqueto*, a suburb below *Tuoro*. Turn right here and walk up the track for a couple of minutes. At this point you arrive at the track lined with cypresses that you walked up earlier **(C)**.

1:47   Turn left near the first cypresses and you are retracing your steps. 4 minutes later you cross a bridge, turn left and cross the second bridge. Continue up *Via Pozzo* and turn right onto *Via Ritorta*. **Note**: at this point you can continue straight on into the town centre where you will find two bars. If you leave out the refreshment option you should be back at the car **(A)** 10 minutes after crossing the second bridge.

Walking time: 2:01

Migianella dei Marchesi: an introduction

The two *Migianella* walks offer the opportunity to explore the abandoned village and castle of *Migianella dei Marchesi*. The name Marchesi suggests that the castle was originally the property of an aristocratic family who controlled a lot of the land and castles in this

Migianella dei Marchesi

area. As the city-states of *Perugia* and *Cortona* became more powerful, the family were forced to concede control of their property. Their descendants, the Del Monte family, ruled the tiny independent state of *Monte Santa Maria Tiberina* near *Città di Castello* until the Napoleonic invasion in 1798.

Until the 1600's, most people in this area lived in fortified settlements called borgos (borghi). Not all borgos have a castle, look out for other clusters of buildings, usually with a church incorporated. Isolated farmhouses were vulnerable to attack by mercenary bands and other lawless groups. *Migianella* castle guarded a route down to *Umbertide*, (known as *La Fratta* before the reunification of Italy). It stands opposite the ruins of the castle at *Sant'Anna* on the other side of the valley.

You can enter the village by taking the path to the right of the castle wall. At the far end of the village you will find a beautiful stone arch and excellent views from a grassy area. There is a ceramic plaque detailing the history of the castle. The castle is thought to have been here since about 1000AD, however, most castles in the *Niccone Valley* are built on the site of earlier fortifications.

The plaque states that cannon was first used here in 1331. It also lists several atrocious acts committed by the neighbouring Tuscans. Among these, it states that the castle was occupied by Florentine troops after the Pazzi conspiracy in 1478 (the pope had backed a

The skeleton of Don Clementini

failed assassination attempt on Lorenzo Medici which succeeded in killing his brother Giuliano).

I heard a rumour that the skeletal remains of a priest had been left in a crate in the confessional of the church before disappearing a few years ago. In October 2005 I met Mike Askins, who has a house close to *Migianella* and has photographs to prove this. The inscription on the crate stated that these were the mortal remains of Don Clementini, the priest at the church between 1863 and 1911 and who was born in *Umbertide* on the 23/11/1827 and died on the 2/11/1911.

To Find The Start

The start of both *Migianella* walks is along an unpaved road off the SS 416 near *Spedalicchio*. The turning is located near the 5km marker.

If you are coming from the direction of *Mercatale*, go through the village of *Spedalicchio*, the road curves sharply right and then left. You pass the 5km marker on your left and a few hundred metres later; you come to a crossroads with a single storey concrete building on the left. Turn right onto the unpaved road. At the time of writing there is a sign advertising the sale of beef (*Spaccio Aziendale di Carne Limousine e Chianina*). This sign may not be here in the future as the Girasole farm have plans to move their butcher's shop to *Molino Vitelli*, 2 km down the road.

Cross a bridge over the *River Niccone*, shortly after you come to a pale yellow house on your right. Go past this house; the road forks immediately after. Take the left fork and park on the left just as the road curves sharply up to the right. There is a green fence on your right.

If you are coming from *Umbertide*, pass through the hamlet of *Molino Vitelli* and continue along the SS 416 for nearly a kilometre after the 4km marker. Look out for a crossroads sign and shortly after this; turn left at the crossroads onto the unpaved road. There is a sign advertising the sale of beef at the turning and a single storey concrete building on the right. Once you are on the unpaved road, follow the directions as above.

2.9 Migianella dei Marchesi: short walk
(allow at least 2 hours)

Walking time: 1 hour 35 minutes. Steep climb but relatively easy terrain, you may need secateurs for one section.

This walk has lovely views of the *Niccone Valley*. It is well worth taking the short extension to the abandoned village and castle of *Migianella dei Marchesi*.

To Find The Start

For directions to the start see **Migianella dei Marchesi, an introduction.**

Walk Synopsis

(A) Starting out on the valley floor, you begin to climb steeply and arrive at a tarmac road.

(B) Continue climbing up the tarmac road.

(C) Take the extension along the unpaved road to *Migianella*.

(D) Return to **(C)**. Descend along the unpaved road to the start **(A)**.

Walk 9: Migianella Short Walk

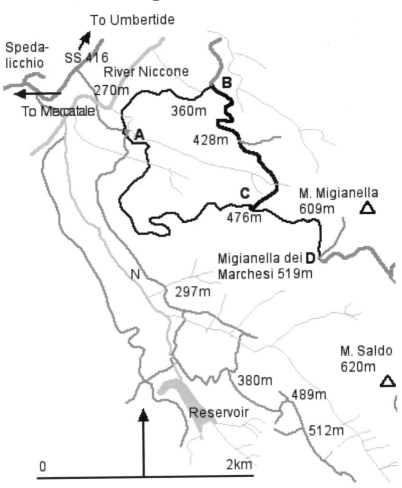

Start (A)

0:00 Walk back the way you came in the car, after 2 minutes you go straight on at the junction and keep going past the pale yellow house on your left. A minute later, the main track bends to the left; take the much smaller track to the right, just after the drive to a house.

0:03 The track runs past the small vineyard in the garden of the house and then through fields. 4 minutes later it forks again. Continue straight on, climbing steeply through a wood. 5 minutes up the track, you pass a restored farmhouse; beyond the house the track becomes rougher and you may need to use your secateurs.

0:12 After 3 minutes you pass a large abandoned farmhouse, follow the track around the house and then take the track to your left. 5 minutes later, you should be at a T-junction with a tarmac road; turn right, heading uphill **(B)**.

0:20 Walk up the asphalt road; there are pines on the right and vines on the left. You pass an old farmhouse and then a modern house quite close to the road on the right. After 8 minutes you pass a group of 3 ruined houses. If you wish, you can enter the field to the right just past these houses and walk beside the road.

0:28 6 minutes after the houses, the road levels out; catch your breath and admire the view to the right. 8 minutes later, the tarmac finishes and the road forks. Just in front is a house built partially of stone and with other areas painted white **(C)**. To take the extension to *Migianella dei Marchesi*, turn left here. To leave out the extension, continue straight on past the house and ignore the next paragraph.

0:42 Immediately after turning left you will see the fortified village (borgo) of *Migianella dei Marchesi* ahead. Behind it you can see *Monte Acuto* and the cross at its summit. 12 minutes later the tarmac road starts again, there is a madonnina to your left and *Migianella dei Marchesi* is to your right **(D)**. You can enter the village by taking the path to the right of the castle wall. After exploring a little (take care, some of the buildings are in a bad state), return the way you came (12 minutes) and take a left at the junction with the house **(C)**.

1:06 Keep going straight on, descending steadily (there are no other tracks to confuse you). Along the way you pass several houses. 27 minutes after the fork, you pass a large house on the left. It has an annexe with several arches. After 2 minutes, you arrive back at your car **(A)**.

Walking time: 1:35

2.10　Migianella dei Marchesi: long walk (allow 4 hours)

Walking time: 2 hours 52 minutes. Relatively hard, steep and rough sections.

This is an updated version of the walk; I had to change the route because a track has been blocked with a locked gate and fencing. The new route crosses a couple of streams and you may get wet feet after exceptionally heavy rain. For directions to the start see **Migianella dei Marchesi, An Introduction**.

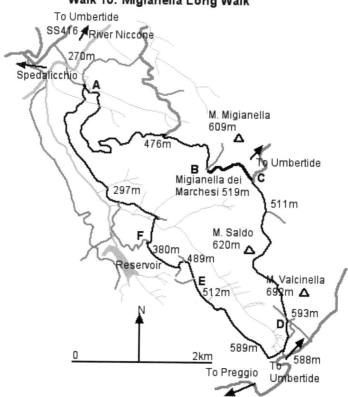

Walk 10: Migianella Long Walk

Walk Synopsis

(A) Climb the unpaved road until you arrive at *Migianella*.

(B) Take the asphalt road from *Migianella* until you arrive at the track lined with pines.

(C) After passing a house the track climbs into the woods emerging to cross a bare plateau.

(D) The track gradually curves around and starts to descend.

(E) Enter woods, continue descending, take a rough track steeply down; follow a low ridge.

(F) Descend from the ridge to the valley floor; follow the track back to the start **(A)**.

Start (A)

0:00 Walk up the unpaved road, after 2 minutes you pass a large house on the right. The green fence encloses the garden of this property. There is an out-building with arches. Continue up the hill for another 30 minutes, passing several houses along the way.

0:32 At this point, the road forks: to the left is a house with walls partially painted white and the rest left as exposed stone (the dogs from the house might bark). Turn right, continuing on the unpaved road (straight on it's tarmaced). Ahead you can see the abandoned castle and village of *Migianella dei Marchesi* with *Monte Acuto* behind it. 11 minutes later, you should be at *Migianella* **(B)**, the fortified wall of the castle is on your right and a madonnina on your left. If you wish to have a look around the village, enter on the path to the right of the wall. Take care as many of the buildings are in a ruinous state.

0:43 From *Migianella dei Marchesi*, continue on the main road, which curves to the left and becomes paved. (Ignore the track on the left going up past the shrine marked by the Club Alpini Italia). From this point, the road is signed with the red and white markers of the Club Alpini Italia (CAI). After 4 minutes, you pass a couple of houses on the right. 5 minutes further on, turn right onto a track lined with pines. There is a CAI sign for path 5D on a pine on the left **(C)**.

0:52 After 5 minutes, you pass a house on your left, a small dog may bark at you. You pass an agricultural building a minute after this.

The path forks immediately after; ignore the left which leads past a ruined house. Take the right track; it is sign-posted 5F by CAI.

0:59 The path starts to climb again and the surroundings become increasingly wooded. After 4 minutes, there are paths leading off to the left and the right. Ignore these and stay on the main track. After another 5 minutes, the climb becomes quite steep. Continue up for another 4 minutes and the track levels and curves to the left.

1:12 The wood starts to thin and after 5 minutes the track emerges onto a bare plateau. There are good views to the left (NE) and right (SW). The path splits but merges again shortly after. After 5 minutes, you come to a junction with five options **(D)**; the fur-thest on the left is a drive through a gate to a house. Consider this as no.1 and count the tracks to the right. Take track no.4, this goes towards a large agricultural building (no.5 almost doubles back in direction and no.2 takes you directly to the start of the Monte Acuto walk should you be masochistic enough to want to join both walks together).

1:22 A minute later, you pass a house on your left and then the large agricultural building on your right. *Monte Acuto* towers above you on the left. Continue for another 7 minutes and you arrive at another junction. Turn right, heading downhill (left will bring you out onto the road between *Umbertide* and *Preggio* close to the start of the *Monte Acuto* walk). After 8 minutes, the road forks next to a large house (Monestevole), take the right. The large St Bernard dog that lives here may bark but otherwise will ignore you. Continue along the track for 14 minutes until the track curves sharply left in front of a large green water tank **(E)**.

1:52 Take the track just to the right of the green water tank; this runs along the right hand side of the olive grove in front of you. It goes between two posts and descends into a wood. A minute later, ignore a track to the right and follow the main track curving to the left. After 2 minutes, ignore another track on the right (this goes down to a gate and into a field) and continue heading around to the left.

1:55   Another 3 minutes along the track, you come to a junction with a path going sharply back to the right. Leave the track going straight on and turn right here. The descent is very steep, so take care. After 5 minutes, you come to a fork, continue straight on. A minute later, you pass a rusting green van. The track follows a low ridge: ignore the minor paths leading off to the left and right.

2:04   3 minutes after the van, you pass a hunter's hide on the right. Another 2 minutes on, the track emerges into a field and runs along the right hand side. A minute later, you are at a fork at the far end of the field; turn right here **(F)**.

2:10   The track descends through a wood. Directly ahead you can see *Migianella* on the hill in front. Three minutes later the path curves left along the edge of a field. Two minutes later you cross a small stream (dry in summer) and the descent levels out. There is a wood on your right and a field on your left.

2:15   Two minutes later a minor path goes to the right; follow the main path which curves left and arrives at a stream less than a minute later. Cross the stream and turn left immediately after. 9 minutes later, the track forks, turn right.

2:26   After 2 minutes you pass between a tobacco tower on your left and a ruined house on your right with a ceramic plaque of the Madonna and Child. After another 12 minutes, you arrive at some large agricultural buildings on your left (the Girasole beef farm), ignore the drive on your right and continue along the main track.

2:40   Another 3 minutes walking and the track curves to the right and goes between two houses. Continue for another 7 minutes and you are at the junction near the yellow house. Turn right and you arrive back at the car in 2 minutes **(A)**.

Walking time: 2:52

2.11 Sant'Anna: short walk
(allow 1 hour 30 minutes)

Walking Time 1 hour 8 minutes. Reasonably easy, can be overgrown in late spring/summer.

The walk starts on the ridge near the ruined church of *Sant'Anna* above the *Niccone Valley.* There are panoramic views aplenty on this relatively easy route. The descent can become overgrown in spring/summer so take long trousers and secateurs at this time of year.

To Find The Start

To get there from *Mercatale*, follow the SS 416 towards *Umbertide.* Go through the village of *Spedalicchio* and take the tarmac road going up on the left just as the main road bends sharply right. There is a small World Wildlife Fund sign for *S.Anna* at the junction. Follow the road up to the ridge, at the top you come to a junction with four options, park here.

Coming from the village of *Niccone*, the road (SS 416) bends sharply right after the 5km sign. Shortly after this, the road bends left and enters *Spedalicchio*. At this point, take the tarmac road on the right. Look for the WWF sign and drive right up to the ridge, (see above).

Walk Synopsis

(A) Walk along the ridge track, includes a short detour to Sant' Anna church.

(B) Descend from the ridge on a path through woods (can be over-grown).

(C) Walk through olive groves and woods until you reach the tarmac road.

(D) Climb back to the start on the tarmac road **(A)**.

Walk 11: Sant'Anna Short Walk

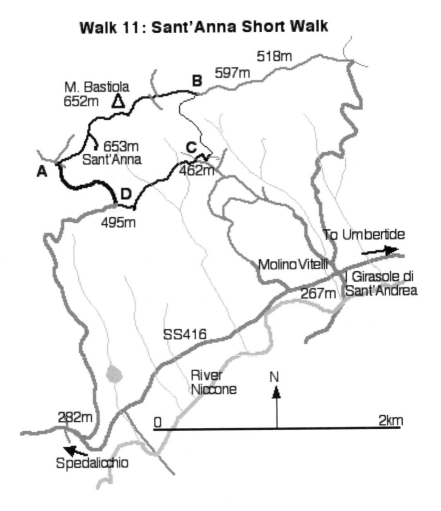

Start (A)

0:00   Stand with your back to road you have just driven up, there is one track on your left and three on your right. Take the middle track of the three on your right. This climbs up into the wood and follows the ridge in an easterly direction; you should spot CAI 5D markers along the way. After 6 minutes, you come to a fork, turn right and take a quick (2 minute) detour up to the ruined church of *Sant'Anna* and a cluster of masts. Faded frescoes are still visible on the exposed inside walls of the church. There is a great view to the south of *Monte Acuto* and *Monte Tezio*. It feels eerie up here, a combination of the ruined building, a madonnina complete with candles, and the hum from the masts' power supply.

0:08   There was also a castle here once; all that remains is the base of the tower. Return down the track (2 minutes) and turn right at the fork, continuing along the ridge and following CAI path 5D. A further 6 minutes along the path, you pass another mast and 4 minutes later yet another one. The road forks a minute after you pass the last mast. Take the left-hand track; this is still CAI 5D, (the right is signed CAI 5E).

0:21   After 2 minutes a minor track joins the track from behind on the left, continue straight on. Another 3 minutes and there is a track on the left with a no entry to vehicles sign, carry straight on. CAI 5D markers should still be visible along the path. Continue for another 2 minutes and then take the path on your right (again signed as path 5E) **(B)**.

0:28   Follow path 5E down, it may be overgrown in spring/summer. After 9 minutes, there is a fence on the left, another 2 minutes and you come to a junction, behind you to your left is a gate leading into the fenced area. Turn right and 2 minutes later turn left at the next junction. Less than a minute later, turn right **(C)**.

0:42   After 2 minutes, you pass a yellow single storey building on the left and the path enters a wood. 3 minutes later ignore minor tracks on the left and right and you emerge into an olive grove. After another 3 minutes, you pass a concrete/metal lock-up on the right and then a drive to a house; follow the track around to the left. Continue for another 3 minutes and the track turns right near a group of houses.

0:53 The track turns into a tarmac road at this point, after 4 minutes; you come to a junction where you turn right **(D)**. A wooden sign for *loc. Riozzo* and a CAI 5D sign on a tree mark this junction. The road climbs up towards the ridge, after 3 minutes, you pass a group of restored houses on the left and right of the road. Another 8 minutes and you arrive back at the car **(A)**.

Walking time: 1:08

2.12   Sant'Anna: long walk
   (allow 2 hours 45 minutes)

Walking time: 2 hours 11 minutes. Reasonably good terrain, a steep climb.

This walk climbs the south facing slopes behind the hamlet of *Molino Vitelli* and up to the ridge. Here you will find the ruins of *Sant'Anna* church and castle next to a cluster of antennae.

To Find The Start

Molino Vitelli is on the SS 416 between the villages of *Spedalicchio* and *Niccone*. Take the turning for the cantina (winery) *Fattoria I Girasole di Sant'Andrea* and park on the road outside. If you buy some wine or use the restaurant, they won't mind you using the car park.

Walk Synopsis

(A) Climb fom *Molino Vitelli* past the *Maridiana Alpaca* farm and on to the next agriturismo (*Pratoverde*).

(B) Continue climbing through olive groves and woods; join a tarmac road taking you up to the ridge.

(C) Follow the ridge track in an easterly direction; there is a quick detour to the church of *Sant'Anna*.

(D) Continue along the ridge.

(E) Descend on the little used tarmac road to *Molino Vitelli* **(A)**.

Walk 12: Sant'Anna Long Walk

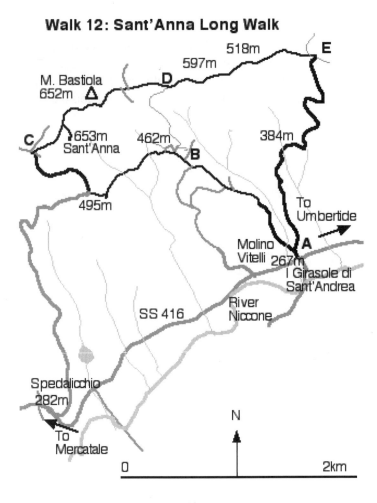

Start (A)

0:00   Cross the main road (the SS 416) and take the road directly opposite. After a minute, the road forks; take the left hand road and follow it up. There are several red and white Club Alpini Italia (CAI) markers for path 5E. After 4 minutes, you pass a house on the left. A further 2 minutes up, you pass a circular tower in the garden of a modern house. A minute beyond the tower, the tarmac ends.

0:08   After 5 minutes, you come to a sign telling you that this is a European Union sponsored alpaca farm for marginal land. Ignore a small track going through a gate on the right. You might see some alpacas (small llamas) in the fields. A minute later, you arrive at a fork next to a group of agriturismo and farm buildings (*Agriturismo Maridiana*).

0:14   Continue straight on past the buildings, the dogs here bark but are quite friendly. (If you are interested, you can arrange a visit to the *Maridiana* farm to see the alpacas and buy clothes made from alpaca and angora wool). 6 minutes later, you come to a junction in front of another agriturismo (*Pratoverde*). Continue straight on, there is a marker for path 5E on a tree **(B)**.

0:20   After another minute ignore a minor track on the right; the *Pratoverde* buildings are still on your left. After a further 2 minutes, ignore a smaller track going up to the right and follow the main track around to the left. Continue for another 2 minutes and you pass a yellow single storey building on the left.

0:25   The track enters a wood and 3 minutes later, emerges with an olive grove on the right, ignore smaller tracks to the left and right. After another 2 minutes, you pass a lock-up on the right and then a drive up to a house. Follow the track to the left and 5 minutes later, you arrive at a group of houses, the track bends sharply right at this point and becomes a tarmac road. 5 minutes later, you come to a T-junction, turn right.

0:40   The road you have just walked up is sign-posted *Loc. Riozzo* and you should be able to spot CAI signs for path 5D on the tree next to it. Follow the tarmac road upwards. 3 minutes later, you pass a group of houses on either side of the road. Another 8 minutes and you arrive at the ridge **(C)**

0:51 Here you have four tracks to choose from, one on the left and three to your right. Take the middle track of the three on your right. This climbs into the wood and follows the ridge in an easterly direction. You should spot CAI 5D markers along the way. After 6 minutes, you come to a fork, turn right and take a quick (2 minutes) detour up to the ruined church of *Sant'Anna* and the cluster of masts.

0:59 There is a great view to the south of *Monte Acuto* and *Monte Tezio*. There is an eerie feeling up here; a combination of the ruined building, a shrine lit with candles, and the hum from the masts' power supply. There was once a castle here, only the base of the tower remains. Return down the track (2 minutes) and turn right at the fork, continuing along the ridge and following CAI path 5D.

1:01 A further 6 minutes along the path, you pass another mast. After another 4 minutes you pass the last mast on the route. The road forks a minute after this; take the left track; this is still CAI 5D, (the right is signed CAI 5E). After another 2 minutes a minor track joins from behind on the left, continue straight on.

1:14 After 3 minutes you pass a track on the left with a no entry to vehicles sign, carry straight on. CAI 5D markers should still be visible along the path. Continue for another 2 minutes and another path signed 5E goes down to the right, ignore this path and continue straight on (still path CAI 5D) **(D)**.

1:19 Continue along path 5D, after a minute ignore a minor path on the left. After 8 minutes, ignore another left hand path. 3 minutes beyond this, the path emerges from the wood into an open field. There is a shed in the trees on the right. Directly ahead (east), you can see *Montone*.

1:31 2 minutes later, you pass a drive to a house on your right. Another 6 minutes and a track joins from the left, continue straight on. Directly ahead on the left is a garden with a pond. The track curves to the right **(E)** and becomes a tarmaced road a minute later.

1:40   Follow the road down to the valley floor, it is not busy and you pass several houses along the way. 30 minutes from the start of the tarmac, you come to a T-junction, turn left. You are now retracing your steps. A minute later, you come to the valley road, cross over and you are back at the car **(A)**.

Walking time: 2:11

2.13 Umbertide and along the Tiber (allow 1 hour 30 minutes)

Walking time: 1 hour 17 minutes. Level easy terrain.

Umbertide is my local town; it has a lovely "centro storico" and a lively weekly market. It's unfortunate that the rest of the town is let down by unimaginative architecture in its sprawling industri-
al and residential zones. If
you do the walk early on a
Wednesday morning, you
should have time to visit the
market when you have
finished.

This walk takes in the old
town before heading along
the banks of the *Tiber* and
then returning through fields.
Although the walk is on low
lying level ground, the wide
Tiber Valley provides an
excellent panorama of the
surrounding hills.

La Rocca

To Find The Start

Parking spaces in the middle of *Umbertide* have an hour time limit and on market day the large unrestricted car park is used for stalls; the best place to park is a small car park just outside the centre on *Via C. Forlanini*. To find the car park, follow signs to *Montone*, and then the hospital, park in the spaces directly opposite the hospital entrance road.

Walk Synopsis

(A) Walk through the town to the path along the *River Tiber*.

(B) Follow the path along the riverbank.

(C) You may have to make a diversion here if the river is high, but quickly rejoin the *Tiber* path. Further on you leave the *Tiber* and follow the bank of the *Carpina*.

(D) Head back towards *Umbertide* passing fields and houses **(A)**.

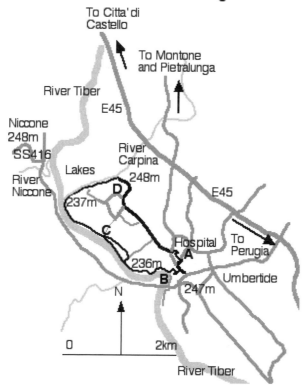

Walk 13: Umbertide and along the Tiber

Start (A)

0:00 Turn left out the car park and walk to the end of *Via C. Forlanini*. Turn left again and follow the road past a row of shops on your left. 3 minutes from the car park, you should be level with the *Rocca*, the imposing tower on your right. Ahead, you can see a large octagonal Renaissance church. Cross the road you are walking along and walk across the car park towards the *Rocca*.

0:03 Pass the *Rocca* on your right and you are funnelled up to a junction with *Via Guidalotti* and *Via Stella*. Turn right onto *Via Stella*; this takes you into the main square, *Piazza Giacomo Matteotti*. Continue across the square and turn right onto *Via Leopoldo Grilli*. This curves left and, after a short descent, you come to a junction with *Via Bovicelli* on the right.

0:07 It is 4 minutes since crossing the road. At this point, take a smaller footpath doubling back on your left behind some railings. The path curves right and a minute later, you come to the path along the *Tiber*. Turn right onto the path and follow the river **(B)**.

0:08 After 14 minutes, you come to a junction. If the water level is low, you can take the left-hand path and follow the riverbank to point **(C)**. However, during the winter, the path is sometimes submerged and you have to turn right.

0:22 If you have to turn right, follow these instructions: After 2 minutes, you come to a junction, turn left onto the tarmac road. After another minute, you pass a house on your right, continue for another 2 minutes and then turn left at the next junction (the road ahead leads to a house), this takes you back down to the river and you rejoin the path **(C)**.

0:27 After 12 minutes, follow the path as it curves right in front of a large channel flowing into the *Tiber*. This is actually the *River Carpina*. On the other side of the channel you can see several rectangular trout fishing lakes. The local pastime of sitting by a featureless pond catching trout may seem a little strange to visitors. The explanation is that there is no need to buy an expensive fishing license.

0:39 After 7 minutes the track forks, take the left and continue alongside the channel (the right goes across a field towards a house).

5 minutes later, you come to a T-junction with an asphalt road; turn right **(D)**.

0:51 After 3 minutes, the track forks next to a house, directly in front you will see some tobacco drying sheds. Take the right-hand track; a further 2 minutes along the road you pass an old farmhouse and several outbuildings. A minute later, you come to a crossroads; turn left here.

0:57 After 5 minutes, you pass a track on your right. Continue for a further 5 minutes and you pass *Via delle Lame* on your right. The frequency of houses (and barking dogs) increase as you approach *Umbertide*.

1:07 After another 5 minutes, you come to the junction with the *Umbertide-Montone* road. Turning right here would take you to the end of *Via C. Forlanini*, however, the road here is extremely narrow and there is no footpath. Instead, turn left and then cross the road almost immediately, this is the back entrance to the hospital.

1:12 When you have walked up the entrance ramp, go through the grey gates. Turn right almost immediately and walk under the part of the hospital directly in front of you. Turn left; go past the entrance to *Pronto Soccorso* (Accident and Emergency) and along the road to the vehicular entrance for the hospital. 5 minutes after crossing the road at the back of the hospital you should be back at your car **(A)**.

Walking time: 1:17

2.14   Rocca d'Aries (Montone short walk, allow 2 hours)

Walking time: 1 hour 38 minutes. A steep climb, some rough terrain.

This walk is dominated by the impressive *Rocca d'Aries*, a castle sitting high on a ridge above the *Carpina Valley*. It was built by the Fortebraccio family (see Montone walk) and gave them control of the area to the east of *Montone*. It has been beautifully restored by the Region of Umbria but strangely, seems to be closed to the public. I don't know for certain but may be possible to arrange a visit through the tourist information office in *Montone*. This walk uses some of the route followed in the *Montone Long Walk*. However, it has a different starting point and, because it starts and ends near the waterfalls, it offers an opportunity for post walk swimming and a picnic.

Rocca d'Aries

To find the start

Drive along the road from *Umbertide* towards *Pietralunga*. Ignore the signs to *Montone* and keep an eye on the kilometre markers along the road. Between the 6 and 7km markers, take a turning on the left sign posted *Osservatorio Astronomico* (Astronomical Observatory) with a board with a map for the *Parco Naturale Alto Tevere* (Upper Tiber Nature Park).

The road crosses two bridges and then you take a right onto a track next to some bins. The observatory is sign posted along the track. Take a kilometre reading at this point; you follow the track for approximately 3km before parking. The track goes past a house on the right; ignore the track going steeply up to the left.

Shortly after the house, the track forks; take the right. The track crosses a bridge; ignore a cypress-lined drive on the left to *Casallina* and cross two more bridges. A word of warning, if there has been exceptionally heavy rain, the bridges may be flooded and, therefore, impassable. After the bridges, the track straightens, keep going.

The track curves left and the *Rocca d'Aries* is clearly visible ahead. The track sweeps around in a broad arc to the right and then curves sharply left again. A little further and you pass a chained track on the left, this leads up to the *Rocca*.

Keep going and a few hundred metres beyond this you arrive at a small lay-by on the right where you park. This spot is marked by a convergence of telephone and electricity poles, the track to the waterfall heads sharply back to the right from the lay-by (if you arrive at a sign on the left pointing up a track to *Pereto*, then you have missed the lay-by and need to turn back).

Walk Synopsis

(A) Climb towards the *Rocca d'Aries*, and then follow the track along a contour of the hillside.

(B) Climbing again, cross the open space to the ridge. Follow the ridge to the *Rocca*.

(C) Continue along the ridge.

(D) Start the descent to the valley floor and follow the track back to the start **(A)**.

Walk 14: Rocca d'Aries

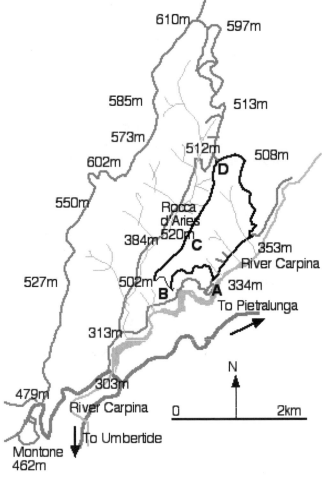

Start (A)

0:00   Head back the way you came, after 2 minutes you take the track on the right with a heavy chain suspended between two upright steel joists. Sometimes, there may be barbed wire stretched across the path to prevent the escape of cattle, it is easy to get past it. After 8 minutes of climbing, you arrive at a house (undergoing restoration at the time of writing). The track forks here; ignore the left to the house and take the right past the tobacco tower.

0:10   It is important to pay attention to the directions at this point; there are many tracks and little to distinguish between them. Immediately after the tobacco tower, the track forks: take the left and start to climb. Two minutes from the tobacco tower the track splits three ways; take the lower path (this is the furthest to the left). The path climbs, after 3 minutes it curves sharply right and emerges onto a small rocky opening.

0:15   Ignore a smaller path to the left (blocked with a barbed wire fence at the time of writing) and follow the main path across the rocks and back into the scrub woodland. Continue for another 2 minutes and the path forks again. Ignore the right (heading uphill), and take the left (descending) path.

0:17   The path goes through thick woods and although it goes up and down in places, it follows a contour around the hillside. In winter, you should be able to make out the route of the track ahead. Far below, you can see the track that you followed in the car along the valley floor; you should now be walking in the opposite direction (west). After 4 minutes, the wood finishes and you come to a large open space covered in broom plants **(B)**.

0:21   At this point, the path turns sharply right and you climb for 4 minutes through the broom. A ruined house is visible on the ridge ahead. The path then turns sharply left and becomes more enclosed; continue to climb for another 2 minutes.

0:27   Finally, you reach the ridge and the path turns sharply right next to a muddy pool. The path widens into a track and after 3 minutes, you pass the ruined house on the right. 3 minutes beyond the house, the *Rocca d'Aries* becomes visible in front. After another 2 minutes, you arrive at a fork in front of the *Rocca,* take the left and you arrive immediately **(C)**.

0:35 When you have finished looking around, continue along the ridge for the next 27 minutes. You should be able to spot the dome of the observatory directly ahead and along the way you pass a newly restored house. When you arrive at a junction with a large outcrop of rock directly in front of you, turn right **(D)**.

1:02 After 6 minutes, you pass a sign on the left for *Casanova*; continue down to the right. Continue for another 16 minutes and you pass a couple of houses on the left. 3 minutes further down, you come to a T-junction with the track along the valley floor; turn right. After 8 minutes, you pass a track going up to *Pereto* on the right. Continue straight on along the valley floor and you arrive back at the car in 3 minutes **(A)**.

Walking time: 1:38

2.15 Montone long walk (allow 6 hours)

Walking time: 4 hours 56 minutes. A steep climb, some rough terrain.

The signs on the road as you approach *Montone* describe it as one of the most beautiful borgos (fortified vilages) in Italy. This is not an exaggeration; the town is well worth a visit. There are fantastic views from many points on the walls, beautiful old streets to wander around and a lively square with two bars.

Montone was home to Andrea Fortebraccio, also known as Braccio Fortebraccio (Arm Strongarm), one of the most feared mercenaries of

Montone with Monte Acuto behind

the early Renaissance period. He was so powerful, that, had he not been killed in Battle in 1424 near *L'Aquila*, he would have been the ruler of central Italy with even the Pope at his command.

The name of the *Rocca d'Aries*, a castle that dominates much of the territory covered on this walk, is linked to the name of *Montone*, which is also the Italian for ram. The remains of another Fortebraccio stronghold can be found at the top of *Montone*. This castle was demolished on the orders of Pope Sixtus IV in 1478 after a descendant of Fortebraccio had allied the town with the Florentines. This occurred against the background of the Pazzi conspiracy, in which the Pope had plotted to remove the Medici family, the rulers of Florence.

To Find The Start

Montone can be reached from the exit on the E45 (just north of *Umbertide*) or directly from *Umbertide* by following the signs (also direction *Pietralunga*). The town is sign posted to the left next to the 2km marker. Follow the road up and park at the first car park just outside the town walls (opposite the *Tre Fonti* Pizzeria). If there has been really heavy rain, it's worth checking the route in your car up to the start of the paragraph headed "0.56" (just after the house called *Casallina*). This is because the bridges may be impassable if the river is really high.

Walk Synopsis

(A) Leave *Montone* and descend on the little used tarmac road.

(B) From the bins follow the white road until you reach the track climbing towards the *Rocca d'Aries*.

(C) Climb towards the *Rocca* and then follow the track along a contour of the hillside.

(D) Climbing again; cross an open space to the ridge. Follow the ridge to the *Rocca*.

(E) Follow the track along the ridge, turn left at a rocky outcrop and then turn right.

(F) Follow the track until it curves sharply left in front of a farmhouse.

(G) Follow the track through woods, rocky landscapes and fields; it feels remote here.

(H) Follow the ridge track back to *Montone* **(A)**.

Walk 15: Montone Long Walk

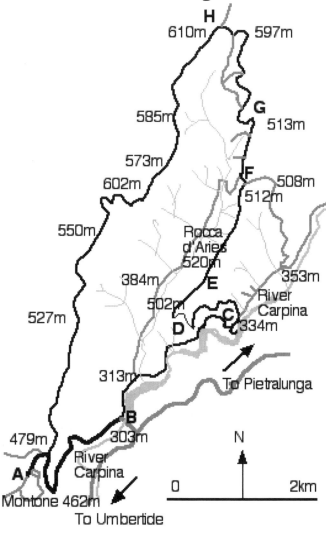

Start (A)

0:00   Leave the car park keeping the town wall on your right, after about 100m the road forks, take the left. This is sign-posted *Pietralunga*, *Carpini* and the *Rocca d'Aries*. Look out for red and white Club Alpini Italia (CAI) signs along the way. 5 minutes from the car park, you pass a small church on your right and a modern looking war memorial. Another 2 minutes and you pass a road on the left sign-posted *La Pieve di San Gregorio*. If you look to the left, you can see the church, which has been incorporated into a farmhouse. Almost immediately, the road curves right and you pass a track on the left sign-posted *Pieve Di Saddi*, you will return along this track at the end of the walk.

0:07   Continue down the tarmac road, after 27 minutes you reach the valley floor and the tarmac road curves sharply right near some bins, **(B)**. At this point, take the unpaved track on the left sign-posted for Perugia University's Observatory (*Osservatorio Astronomico*). After 8 minutes, ignore a minor track going up to the left next to some metal sheds. Straight after this, you pass a house and a reservoir (where the river has been dammed) is visible on your right. 3 minutes later, you come to a fork, take the right hand track.

0:45   Continue along the track, after 2 minutes, you cross a bridge with a CAI marker. 3 minutes later, you pass a track on the left going to a house called *Casallina*. After another 3 minutes, the track dips; you then cross two bridges in the next 3 minutes.

0:56   For the next 8 minutes, the track is fairly straight, ignore minor tracks on the right leading down to the right, the track then curves sharply left and the *Rocca d'Aries* is visible on the ridge ahead. Keep following the track for another 10 minutes and just before you go around a second sharp left bend, you can see the *Rocca d'Aries* directly behind you.

1:14   Continue along the valley floor for another 4 minutes, you now take a track on your left, the route up to the *Rocca*. This is a steep, but fairly well made track, with a heavy chain hung between two posts made from upended steel joists. Further distinguishing features are the woodland on the left and pasture on the right. **(C)** In addition to the chain, there may be barbed wire stretched across the path to prevent the escape of cattle, it is easy to get past it.

1:18 **Note:** Should you wish to make a small diversion to a waterfall, continue along the main track for 2 minutes and take the track on the right down to the river, to continue the walk afterwards, return the way you came and turn right up the track.

After 8 minutes of climbing, you arrive at a house (undergoing restoration at the time of writing). The track forks here; ignore the left to the house and take the right past the tobacco tower. It is important to pay attention to the directions at this point; there are many tracks and little to distinguish between them.

1:26 Immediately after the tobacco tower, the track forks: take the left and start to climb. Two minutes from the tobacco tower, the track splits three ways, take the lower path, this is the furthest to the left. The path climbs and after 3 minutes curves sharply right and emerges onto a small rocky opening.

1:31 Ignore a smaller path to the left (blocked with a barbed wire fence at the time of writing) and follow the main path across the rocks and back into the scrubby woodland. Continue for another 2 minutes and the path forks again. Ignore the right (heading uphill), and take the left, descending path. The path goes through thick woods, although it goes up and down, it generally follows a contour around the hillside.

1:33 In winter, you should be able to make out the route of the track ahead. Far below, you can see the track that you followed along the valley floor; you should now be walking in the opposite direction (west). After 4 minutes, the wood finishes and you come to a large open space covered in broom plants **(D)**.

1:37 At this point, the path turns sharply right and you climb for 4 minutes through the broom. A ruined house is visible on the ridge ahead. The path then turns sharply left and becomes more enclosed; continue to climb for another 2 minutes. Finally, you reach the ridge and the path turns sharply right next to a muddy pool.

1:43   The path widens into a track and after 3 minutes; you pass the ruined house on the right. 3 minutes beyond the house, the *Rocca d'Aries* becomes visible in front. After another 2 minutes, you arrive at a fork in front of the *Rocca*, take the left and you arrive immediately **(E)**.

1:51   When you have finished looking around, continue along the ridge for the next 27 minutes. You should be able to spot the dome of the observatory directly ahead. When you arrive at a junction with a large outcrop of rock directly in front of you, turn left. After another 2 minutes, the track forks again, take the right **(F)**.

2:20   After 5 minutes, you pass a track to some farmhouses on the left, another 4 minutes and the track forks; take the right that leads directly towards a farmhouse (and looks as if it might end there). After 2 minutes, you arrive at the farmhouse; the track curves to the left in front of the house and then forks immediately. Take the left-hand path; there is a CAI 3C marker on an electricity pole right at the start of the path **(G)**.

2:31   After 2 minutes you come to a junction; turn right. After another 2 minutes the track becomes muddy and you pass a spring on your left (if you are walking in the summer this may, of course, have dried up). Continue for a further 3 minutes and the path crosses an open, rocky space. You will probably notice a CAI marker on a small oak tree growing between the rocks; the path climbs and goes back into the woods.

2:38   After 6 minutes, another track joins from the left; continue straight on and 2 minutes later the path curves sharply right and heads across fields towards an abandoned house. In 2 minutes, you reach the house, the track curves sharply left around the house and a minute later you come to a junction. A track joins from behind to the right and the main track continues straight uphill, there is also another, less well made track going off at 90^0 to the right. Take this track, after less than a minute you should see a faint CAI marker on a gatepost.

2:49 9 minutes from the junction, the track curves sharply left in front of a house and climbs uphill alongside the fence. When you get to the top (2 minutes later), turn left and head away from the house. After 3 minutes, a track joins from the left; continue straight on. In another 3 minutes, you come to a T-junction, turn left here **(H)**.

3:06 The track runs along the ridge or just below it, until you reach *Montone*, nearly 2 hours walk away. Stay on the main track, (there are a few turnings going to houses and off into the woods) and 1 hour 43 minutes later, (if you walk at the same speed as me!) you arrive back at the tarmac road on which you left Montone. Turn right and retrace your steps to the car, you should arrive around 7 minutes later **(A)**.

Walking time: 4:56

After completing this walk, a well-deserved drink in the main square of *Montone* is called for. Head up the steps on your left and through the *Del Verziere* gate; a short walk up the street leads you into the square. For anyone who simply cannot face this short, but steep climb, drive your car around the outside of the walls and see if you can park just beyond the next gate, this allows access at the same level as the square.

2.16 Monte Acuto (allow 3 hours)

Walking time: 2 hours 16 minutes, steep climbs and descents, rough terrain, can become overgrown in spring/summer in places, take secateurs.

Monte Acuto is an unusually angular mountain compared to those around it, hence I suppose, its name. At the risk of sounding pedantic, the angle seems to me to be greater than 90^0, so perhaps *Monte Ottuso* would be a more appropriate if less dramatic name. Anyone who has spent time in *Umbertide* will undoubtedly have noticed it and the cross at its summit to the south west of the town.

Etruscan bronze statues have been found at the top, it seems that there was a temple here, I think the fenced in stone walls are connected to this site. The walk to the summit is a tough climb. Descending, although not quite at the same gradient, is also steep. In spring and summer, the narrow path near the end of the walk can become overgrown; it is a good idea to take long trousers and secateurs if you do the walk at this time of year. In the warmer months, cattle may be grazing on the pasture at the top of the mountain. Near the end of the walk, there is a very narrow stretch of path across a steep rock-face. This outing is not for the unfit or sufferers of vertigo. However, if you are physically up to the challenge, you will be rewarded with great views at the summit.

To Find The Start

The start of this walk is just off the road between *Preggio* and *Umbertide*. If you are coming from *Umbertide*, this road is opposite the ERG garage and leads under the railway. There are two roads here, so make sure you take the one sign-posted *Preggio*. Ignore the sign for the hamlet of *Monte Acuto* and follow the road past the large disused quarry in the side of the mountain. Just before you reach the 7km marker, take the track on the left and park.

Coming from *Castel Rigone* or *Preggio*, follow signs to *Umbertide* and turn right onto the track just after the 7km marker. Look out for a red and white Club Alpini Italia (CAI) 5A marker on a tree to the right of the track.

Walk Synopsis

(A) Climb up into the woods, passing above the disused quarry.
(B) The path emerges from the woods and continues to climb steeply
to the summit.
(C) Descend from the summit to the other side of the mountain.
(D) The track starts to take you back towards the start around the
side of the mountain.
(E) Continue back to **(A)** on narrow paths and wider tracks.

Walk 16: Monte Acuto

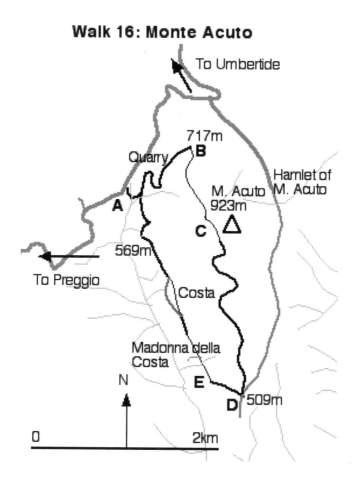

Start (A)

0:00 Follow the track, after 1 minute it forks, follow the left (main) track and 2 minutes later it forks again. Take the left track which heads uphill (you will return on the track to the right). The track enters a pinewood and climbs above the disused quarry. Continue for 20 minutes and you reach a small clearing with a pile of stones over a fireplace **(B)**.

0:23 Take a path going up to the right into the wood; this is marked by red arrows sprayed on the side of an oak tree and at intervals along the path. After 6 minutes, the wood starts to open out and the path divides in two; follow the upper path. A minute later, you take a sharp left onto a rough path marked by arrows on the stones in front of you (you may have to look closely to find the arrow as the cows have churned up the ground).

0:30 The path almost doubles back on itself at this point; after a couple of minutes it curves around to the right and becomes rougher and even less defined. Red arrows continue to mark the way occasionally. The track then levels out and crosses a high pasture. The views continue to get better as you approach the summit. This is clearly visible in front, marked with antennae and large cross. Look out for kestrels hovering on the updraft.

0:32 After 20 minutes, you arrive at the top **(C)**; the views all around are fantastic. To the west you can see a glimpse of *Lake Trasimeno*, *Monte Amiata* and the hill town of *Montepulciano*. To the north, you can make out *Monte Santa Maria Tiberina*, *Città di Castello* and *Montone*. To the east are the *Appenines* and to the south lie *Monte Tezio* and *Monte Subasio*.

0:52 From the summit **(C)**, walk to the right of the fenced in antennae and follow the track down from the mountain. At various points, short cuts allow you to take a steeper route down, I prefer to ignore these and take the longer, shallower route. 35 minutes later, you arrive at the bottom **(D)**; there is a green barrier (often left open). The track forks almost immediately afterwards, take the right hand track.

1:27 Follow the track; it is regularly marked with CAI 5A signs. After 7 minutes, it enters a wood and curves to the left. There are 5A markers on a rock on the right and then on a tree. Just after the CAI marked tree, take a narrow path going up to the right marked with red arrows **(E)**. This path is reasonably hard to spot but should you miss it, the main track peters out shortly afterwards near a ruined house. If you arrive at the ruin turn around and continue looking for the path (now on your left).

1:34 This path is narrow and often has a steep drop on your left. At times, it almost seems to be overgrown but keep going and it will open up again. You may need to use your secateurs here (if you packed them). After 10 minutes you come to the first ruin along the path, the church of *Madonna della Costa*. 5 minutes later you arrive at a house (undergoing restoration in spring 2005). Go through the garden (there is a right of way which will hopefully be restored as a path) and the route widens into a track.

1:49 Continue for another 4 minutes and the main track curves sharply left (sufferers of vertigo may prefer to stay on the main track at this point and so avoid crossing the steep rock face); take the narrow path on the right going up into the woods. 5 minutes later the path narrows as you cross a steep rock face (the costa, or slope that the church is named after), 2 minutes beyond this, you arrive at the first of a group of three houses. You may need to get the secateurs out again along this section.

2:00 Another 2 minutes along the path, you pass the other two ruins and the path rejoins the track. Continue for another 12 minutes and you arrive at a junction, turn left and you are now retracing your steps. 2 minutes later, you arrive back at the car **(A)**.

Walking time: 2:16

2.17 Monte Tezio (allow 2 hours)

Walking time: 1 hour 30 minutes, a hard climb.

At 961m, the summit of *Monte Tezio* offers a fantastic 360^0 view of *Umbria* and southern *Tuscany*. The climb to the top is hard but well worth the effort. At weekends the nature reserve may be busy with walkers from nearby *Perugia*. In theory, hunting is not permitted on *Monte Tezio*. In the warmer months you may encounter cattle on the pasture at the summit.

To Find The Start

From the SS 75 between *Perugia* and *Magione*, take the *Mantignana* exit. Keep on the main road past *Mantignana* and then turn right for *Colle Umberto*. Go through *Colle Umberto* and then turn right onto the road for *Monte Tezio* and *Compresso*.

The road climbs steeply between olive groves and houses. After 2.5 kilometres you arrive at a T-junction, turn right, there is a sign for car parking to the right. The main car park is here, but you can continue up in the car and park near the gate to the nature reserve. This avoids 5 minutes' walk through a residential area.

From the E45 between *Perugia* and *Umbertide*, take the *Pierantonio* exit and follow the signs for *Corciano* and *Magione*. You pass a large castle on the right and go straight over a crossroads at the village of *Pantano*. A few kilometres after *Pantano*, turn left for *Maestrello* (part of the sign is missing at the time of writing). Just as you enter the next village of *Colle Umberto* take the left for *Monte Tezio* and *Compresso*. Follow the directions in the previous paragraph.

Walk Synopsis

(A) Enter the nature reserve and climb along the track.
(B) Take path no.1, which winds up into the woods.
(C) Emerge from the woods and cross the pasture to the summit of *M. Tezio.*
(D) From the summit you follow a path (faint at times) to *Croce della Pieve.*
(E) Locate the narrow path and follow it down to **(B)**. Retrace your steps to the car **(A)**.

Walk 17. Monte Tezio

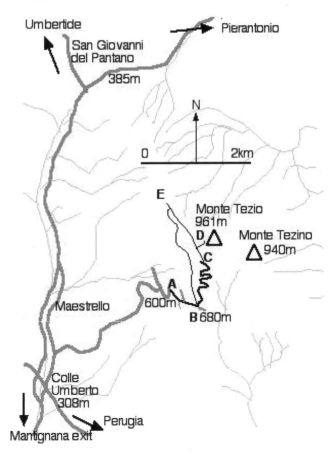

Start (A)

0:00 Pass the gate on the left and walk up the track into the woods. Just after the gate you pass a large wooden map and another board informing you of the nature reserve regulations. After 4 minutes you arrive at a fork. Stay on the main track to the left. 1 minute later, ignore a path joining from the left; you then pass a board with information on the local flora.

0:05 Walk a further 5 minutes and you arrive at a single storey stone building **(B)**. There are three options here. Ignore a small path marked with a red and white sign of the Club Alpini Italia (CAI) going up some steps to the left of the building (it is labelled path no.3 and is the path that you return on). In front of you, the track splits; take the left. A small wooden board to your left tells you that this is CAI path no.1.

0:10 The path climbs up through several hairpin bends. After 7 minutes, you pass a minor track on the left. Another 5 minutes climbing, and you pass another track on the left; follow the main route which twists sharply right and upwards. 7 minutes later the path emerges from the woods onto a high pasture. **(C)**

0:29 Take the track heading across the field straight towards the ridge in front of you. This path then divides; take the right continuing towards the ridge. 3 minutes after entering the field, you cross the ridge and the summit of Monte Tezio (961m) is visible in front of you on your right. 4 minutes from the ridge leave the main track and follow a fainter and narrower path to the right. There is red paint on a stone marking this junction; this path takes you directly to the summit.

0:36 You should arrive 2 minutes later, passing a stone marker along the way; there is a pile of stones marking the top of *Monte Tezio* **(D)**. The view here is outstanding; to the southeast you can see *Perugia, Monte Subasio, Assisi* and the nearby peak of *Monte Tezino* (940m), recognisable straight away due to the large antenna. *Lake Trasimeno* lies directly to the west and the *Appenines* run down the entire eastern view. In fact, everywhere you look, hills and mountain ranges stretch into the distance. Suddenly, the hard climb through the woods seems worthwhile. Look to the north and you should see the cross at *Croce della Pieve* (sideways on so it looks more like a pole), this is where you are heading next.

0:38 Return the way you came and 2 minutes later; turn right onto the wider path at the junction. After another 2 minutes, turn left at a fork. On your left, you pass a hollow filled with scrub vegetation which has taken advantage of the more sheltered conditions; CAI markers now sign the way. It is a short climb (2 minutes) to the next ridge; the path then dips down and climbs towards a rocky area.

0:44 4 minutes later the path passes to the right of the main group of rocks. It then becomes fainter and rockier, look out for CAI markers painted onto stones. After 3 minutes, the path bends sharply to the left and then turns right along a ridge. Further along the ridge a large cross is visible, 4 minutes later, you should reach it, *Croce della Pieve* (942m). **(E)**

0:55 Stop to admire another fine view and retrace your steps for about 100 metres. You are looking for a fairly distinct but very narrow path going down and ahead to the right. In September 2005 it was marked with a wooden stake, but I can't guarantee that this will be there forever. Hopefully, you should find it within a minute, take the path and start the descent.

0:56 After 3 minutes, the path divides; take the left. A minute later you pass a large rock-face on your left, the path passes between blackthorn bushes. 3 minutes further on, the path emerges from the blackthorn and runs near to a barbed wire fence. 2 minutes later, the path joins another path cutting diagonally across it. Turn right here (downhill) and pass through the fence. Stay on the main path, always heading downhill.

1:05 After 5 minutes, ignore a path going to the right as the main route curves sharply left. 2 minutes later you re-enter the woods. As you descend, ignore a couple of tracks on the left (both go up). After 12 minutes, you arrive back at the single storey stone building **(B)**. Turn right and retrace your steps, 6 minutes later you arrive back at the car **(A)**.

Walking time: 1:30

2.18 Perugia City Walk (allow 2-3 hours)

Walking time: 56 minutes, lots of steps and some steep climbs.

Perugia is the capital of *Umbria* but is often overlooked by tourists heading for nearby *Assisi*. Anyone attempting to enter the city by car will soon start to feel that the Perugians are determined to prevent visitors from reaching their amazing medieval city centre. For this reason

Piazza IV Novembre - Palazzo dei Priori and the Fontana Maggiore

I have included detailed instructions to help you negotiate the one-way system and its seemingly arbitrary sign posting.

The walk includes several stops and the actual time will be much longer than the stated walking time. I suggest aiming to arrive at about

9.30 in the morning; this leaves plenty of time to visit the *Collegio di Cambio*, the *Etruscan Well* and the church of *San Severo* before they shut for lunch.

To Find the Car Park "Parcheggio Partigiani"

First get to the *Prepo* exit on the motorway around *Perugia*, have a look at a map before you set off because the roads from different directions join in some fairly bizarre junctions with limited sign posting. If you are coming from *Umbertide*, *Assisi* or *Todi*, keep following signs for *Perugia* and the exit is directly after the second tunnel. If you are coming from the direction of *Lake Trasimeno*, you go through several tunnels and *Prepo* is the junction after *San Faustino*.

Once at the *Prepo* exit, the task of finding the *Centro Storico* begins. At times, you may see signs for the *Centro* pointing in different directions to my instructions; ignore them. If you have come from the direction of the *Lake*, turn right at the end of the slip road and pass under the motorway. Traffic from the other direction feeds into the road at this point and there is an obligatory right turn around the *Perugia Plaza Hotel*.

Once around the hotel, move across into the left-hand lane and continue to the T-junction at the top with traffic lights. Turn left here and get into the right hand lane. The right lane feeds around to the right (uphill again), next to a sign for the *Centro*. Continue uphill until you come to a traffic light with a no-entry sign ahead of you. Turn left here (there is also a sign for the *Piazzale Europa* car park). Get into the right hand lane and you come to a T-junction on a sweeping curve; turn right here.

Keep going for the next 1.2km along the tree-lined road (ignore signs for the *Piazzale Europa* car park). The road briefly becomes single lane and one-way before opening out into 3 lanes. Get into the left-hand lane and shortly after, turn left into the *Parcheggio Partigiani*, (Partisans' Car Park). You may have to wait a few minutes to get in.

Walk Synopsis

(A) From the car park head up into the *Underground City*.

(B) Leave the underground city and follow the *Corso Vannucci* to the *Palazzo dei Priori*.

(C) After exploring the *Collegio del Cambio* head to the *Piazza IV Novembre*.

(D) A short walk takes you to the *Etruscan Well*.

(E) Another short walk takes you to *San Severo* and an early fresco by Raphael.

(F) Head through narrow alleys to a great view from *Piazza Gio Battista Rossi Scotti*.

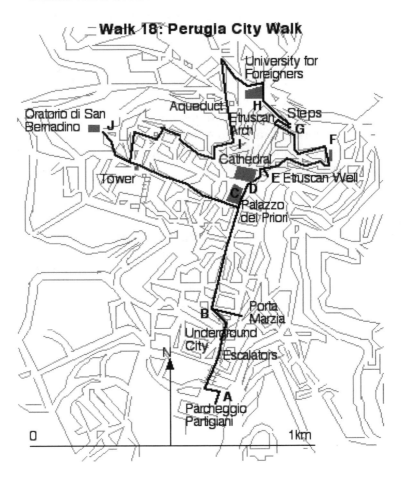

Walk 18: Perugia City Walk

(G) Go down some steps and arrive at the *Etruscan Arch*.

(H) Go past the *University for Foreigners* and climb the medieval aqueduct.

(I) Head through streets and alleys arriving at the *Oratorio di San Bernardino*.

(J) Climb back to the *Corso Vannucci* **(C)**. Visit the *Galleria Nazionale dell' Umbria* and then return via **(B)** to the car park **(A)**.

Start (A)

0:00 Leave the car park, (take your ticket with you) and head for the pedestrian exit, walk straight along the underground corridor following signs for *Centro* and *Scala Mobile* (escalator). At the end of the corridor, turn left onto an escalator. Immediately after this, go up a ramp directly in front of you. Turn right and go up the next escalator, at the top, you walk past some market stalls; it is now 3 minutes since you left the car park. Follow the footpath, you enter a tunnel and ride a series of escalators taking you up. 4 minutes from the stalls you arrive in the *Underground City* **(B)**.

The Underground City

0:07 The *Underground City* is an extraordinary sight, vaulted brick ceilings have been constructed over medieval streets, houses and churches. This is all that remains of the *Rocca Paolina*, the papal fortress built to subdue the city by Pope Paul III. In 1540 the Pope deliberately provoked the Perugians, who were led by the bloodthirsty Baglioni family, into a revolt. He achieved this by breaking his promise not to raise the tax on salt. In doing so, he could finally end the city's independence from *Rome*. He could also avenge himself of the murder of a Papal envoy, commited six years earlier by a member of the Baglioni family. The Papal army quickly captured the city and once all the nuns of the city had kissed his feet the Pope built the *Rocca Paolina* straight over the houses of the Baglioni and their neighbours.

The *Rocca Paolina* was torn down in 1860, when Garibaldi liberated the city from Papal control. A year earlier, the Swiss Guard massacred around two thousand citizens who were participating in a pro-unification demonstration. After Garibaldi had captured *Perugia*, the Papal soldiers were escorted out of the city to prevent the citizens from getting their revenge.

At the top of the escalators, turn right down *Via Bagliona*, the underground street. After a minute you emerge through a door into the open air, walk down the steps and then turn around. The door you walked through is set into an arch, the *Porta Marzia* (Gate of Mars). The lower blocks date back to the Etruscans and the upper part is Roman. The Pope's architect, Sangallo the Younger, liked the arch so much that he dismantled it and incorporated it into the walls of the fortress. Originally, it would have been the city's southern entrance.

0:08 Return through the gate and make your way back up *Via Bagliona*. You can spend a while wandering around the fortress. Once you have finished, go straight past the escalators that you arrived on, and you come to another escalator going up to the right. This takes you up to *Piazza Italia*; all the buildings here date to the period after the demolition of the *Rocca Paolina*, the 1860's and 70's.

0:10 If you came straight here from the *Porta Marzia*, the walking time is 2 minutes. Cross the large grassed roundabout in the middle of *Piazza Italia* and head straight towards the wide pedestrian street directly in front of you. This is the *Corso Vannucci*, named after Perugia's most famous painter, Pietro

Vannucci (also known as Perugino). The width of this road is exactly the same as the main streets found in excavations of Etruscan settlements.

0:12   After 2 minutes, you should be alongside the most impressive building in Perugia, the Palazzo dei Priori, (the medieval city hall and still seat of local government today) **(C)**. The size and grandeur of the building is testimony to Perugia's wealth as an independent city-state in the period before Papal rule.

0:14   It's time for a break, I recommend *Bar Sandri* on your right (closed Mondays), easily recognisable by the impressive display of chocolate cakes in the window. If the weather is nice, sit at a table in the street and a waiter will come out and serve you. The hot chocolate (cioccolata calda) is made on the premises and is not to be missed. There are no toilets in the bar, if you need to go, look for a WC sign pointing down a street just to the left of the *Palazzo dei Priori*.

The Collegio del Cambio and the Collegio della Mercanzia

Now it is time for some serious art. A small door in the *Palazzo dei Priori* (opposite *Bar Sandri*) leads to the *Collegio del Cambio* (open Mon-Sat 0900-1230 1400-1730 Sun 0900-1230), the meeting rooms of the moneychangers' guild. The main room contains the finest frescoes by Perugino (Pietro Vannucci) in *Perugia*. It's worth buying the more expensive ticket; this allows you to visit the chamber of the merchants' guild (*Collegio della Mercanzia*) afterwards.

A fresco is painted straight onto a thin layer of fresh (fresco) plaster; the paint is actually absorbed into this surface. It is skilled work as mistakes are hard to rectify and the plaster has to be painted before it dries (the artist prepares a small section of fresh plaster each day). The frescoes in the *Collegio del*

Cambio compare figures from Greek and Roman history and mythology with their biblical counterparts. For good measure, astrological symbols are thrown into the overall design on the ceiling. The linking of pagan and Christian symbols and ideas was common in the 15th Century (Perugino received the commission in 1499).

Renaissance thinkers looked back to the civilisations of *Greece* and *Rome* to rediscover the knowledge lost in the Dark Ages. In the 1500's, the threat to the Papacy from Protestantism lead to a much narrower, strictly Christian view of what was acceptable in works of art. In the middle of the south wall, there is a self-portrait of a well fed Perugino in a red hat and painted to look as if it is a picture hanging on the wall. Incidentally, a very young Raphael may have assisted Perugino with these frescoes, although there is no documented evidence. It is thought that Raphael could have been the model for the prophet Daniel.

There is a chapel dedicated to St. John the Baptist beyond this room; the frescos are not by Perugino and the quality is not as high, although children usually enjoy looking at the gruesome picture of St. John's decapitation. On leaving the *Collegio del Cambio*, turn left and walk past the main entrance to the Palazzo, a large Gothic arch, and look for another, much smaller door. This is the entrance to the *Collegio della Mercanzia* (open Mon-Sat 0900-1230 1400-1730 Sun 0900-1230), the chambers of the merchant's guild. Use your ticket from the *Collegio del Cambio* to enter. The room doesn't take long too look around but is decorated with impressive wooden panelling and inlays.

Piazza IV Novembre

Turn left on leaving the *Collegio del Cambio* and a minute later you are in the *Piazza IV Novembre*, the centre of the city **(D)**.

The *Duomo* and the *Palazzo dei Priori* face each other across the square. The Piazza is dominated by a medieval fountain, the *Fontana Maggiore*. It dates to 1277 and was made by the sculptors Nicola Pisano and his son Giovanni.

Art historians often cite the realistic style (influenced by Greek and Roman sculpture) of these sculptors when they look to the roots of the Renaissance and the end of the Gothic. Gothic is the Northern European medieval style; the name is derived from a sneering association in the mind of Renaissance man with barbarian invaders from the north.

Again, Christian symbolism is freely mixed with astrological signs and Greek and Roman mythology. Look for the signs of the zodiac and the corresponding labour of the month, (locals still kill their pigs in December). Others to look out for are the lion and griffin (the symbol of Perugia). Scenes from Roman legends and Aesop's fables can be found next to the biblical images of the Garden of Eden and Samson and Delilah, as well as representations of science and the arts. The upper basin has statues representing *Perugia* and the surrounding countryside. Walk around the fountain and the corners of the panels on the upper and lower basins never converge, this is deliberately intended to draw your eye around it.

Take a look at the façade of the *Duomo*. The arches on the left, the *Loggia di Braccio Fortebraccio*, were built in 1423 by the powerful mercenary and Lord of Perugia of the same name (see *Montone* walks). Unless you have a particular interest in Italian cathedrals, the interior is not worth exploring.

The pulpit to the right of the entrance was specially built for the Franciscan preacher, San Bernadino di Siena. He was so popular that the crowds could not fit into the *Duomo* and he addressed them in the square. Later on in the walk, you come to the *Oratorio di San Bernadino,* a church dedicated to his memory. The statue of the Pope, Julius III, may seem a little strange in a city where the Papacy was so unpopular; he did away with many of the harsh taxes that Paul III imposed on the city and was the one Pope that the Perugians liked.

Pozzo Etrusco (Etruscan Well)

0:15 Leave the square to the right of the *Duomo*. This takes you into *Piazza Dante*, cross the road on your right (this is disguised as a pedestrian area until you notice the cars) and 2 minutes from *Piazza IV Novembre*, you will come to the entrance to the *Etruscan Well*. Look for a sign for the *Pozzo Etrusco* **(E)** above the entrance to an alley on your right.

0:17 Walk down the alley and a go in the entrance door on your left. Keep your ticket, it will also allow you access to the next point of interest on the walk, the fresco at the church of *San Severo*. If it is a busy day, you may have to wait a while because only six people are allowed on the bridge over the well at any one time. The well is huge, and supplied the whole of the city with water in Etruscan times; it would seem that Roman engineering skills developed with Etruscan knowledge.

San Severo

When you leave the *Etruscan Well*, turn right at the end of the alley and walk across the right side of *Piazza Piccinino*. Look for the wellhead on your left; you were standing under it a few minutes ago. You enter *Via Bontempi* and 2 minutes after leaving the *Pozzo Etrusco*, take a left up *Via Raphaello*, a narrow street. A minute later, you arrive at the next point of interest on the walk, the church of *San Severo* **(F)**.

0:20 In a side-chapel of the church, you will find a fresco started by the young Raphael and finished after his death by Perugino, his former teacher. Before he had completed the fresco,

Raphael was called to *Rome* and left it unfinished. In 1521, a year after Raphael died; Perugino finished the fresco, already aware that his former pupil had outshone him. The difference between the top and bottom of the frescoes is noticeable, Perugino was clearly in decline in his final years; think of the frescoes he painted at the height of his career in the *Collegio del Cambio*.

Turn right as you come out of the chapel, *Via Raphaello* turns into *Via dell'Aquila*, this is a short stretch under some vaults and then you take a left up the steps of a narrow alleyway. 3 minutes from *San Severo*, you arrive in the triangular *Piazza Biordo Michelotti* (look for the sign behind you on your left). Take the road down to the right out of the piazza, after a minute, the road curves left and you come to *Piazza Gio Battista Rossi Scotti* **(G)**. Piazza seems to be a bit of an exaggeration; it is little more than a road with a wide pavement. However, along the edge of the piazza, there is a fantastic view of rooftops, churches, walls and hills. Don't lean too far over the wall, it's a long drop below.

Arco Etrusco (Etruscan Arch)

0:24 Once you have finished admiring the view, continue along the piazza and head down the wide steps directly in front of you. The steps double back on themselves a couple of times and 2 minutes later, you come to a junction with a steep road. Turn right and follow the steps down. A minute later you arrive at the busy *Piazza Fortebraccio*. Cross the road you have just walked down, pass a fountain on your left and you come to the *Arco Etrusco* (*Etruscan Arch*); the most impressive entrance to *Perugia* **(H)**.

0:27 To properly admire the arch, walk straight past it and cross the road on your right. A minute after arriving at the piazza, you should be standing on the path outside the large red brick building, the *Università dei Stranieri* (*University for Foreigners*), this is the best place to get a good view. The large stone blocks at the bottom are Etruscan, dating to the 2nd Century BC, the top part of the arch is Roman and the loggia on the top left is Renaissance.

If you visit the *Galleria Nazionale Dell' Umbria* at the end of the walk, you will see a fresco of *Perugia* painted before the loggia was added. Note the inscription "Augusta Perusia" at the top of the arch. The Emperor Augustus captured the city in the power struggle following the death of Julius Ceasar; note the size of the lettering, clearly the emperor considered himself to be far more important than the city.

A Medieval Aqueduct

0:28 Turn around and walk away from the arch, keeping the *University for Foreigners* on your left. Turn left onto *Via Ariodante Fabretti*, the footpath along here is narrow and then finishes altogether. Traffic is only allowed in one direction at a time along this stretch. After maybe 200m without the footpath, turn left onto the pedestrian *Via Aquedotto* It is 2 minutes since you left the *University for Foreigners*.

0:30 *Via Aquedotto* was a medieval aqueduct carrying water to the *Fontana Maggiore*, the medieval fountain you saw earlier on. You may be surprised to see that the water flowed uphill; the water was piped from a source higher than the fountain. The siphoning action was aided by a steady reduction in the pipe diameter; this increased the water pressure along the length of the aqueduct.

Walking along the aqueduct is a wonderful experience. You can look down into gardens and onto rooftops and should you wish, straight into houses. At the time of writing, there is a rude message on one fridge to confront those looking in. I'm not sure it has the desired effect, since I look out for it every time! The aqueduct ends in a set of steps. 8 minutes from the start of *Via Aquedotto*, you arrive at the top **(I)**; turn right onto *Via Baldeschi*.

0:38   *Via Baldeschi* leads to *Piazza Felice Cavalotti* almost straight away. Continue in the same direction over the piazza and then along *Piazza Morlacchi* (again, this is more of a road than a piazza). After 2 minutes, you come to a junction in front of the *Uffici Tributi* (Tax Office). Turn right here and then immediately left onto *Via Aquilone*, you then pass a building on your right called the *Università Degli Studi* (*University of Studies*).

0:40   One minute later, turn left onto *Via Francolina* and then immediately right onto *Via della Tartaruga* (Tortoise Street). 2 minutes later, turn left at the end of *Via della Tartaruga* and after about 20 metres, turn right down some steps. You have to turn left at the bottom of the steps onto *Via delle Siepe*. The sign is at the far end of the street; when you get there it is 3 minutes from the top of the steps. Turn right and a minute later you will find yourself facing two churches with a large grassed area in front.

The Oratorio di San Bernardino

0:47   In good weather, this is a popular meeting place for students from the University. The smaller church on the left is the *Oratorio di San Bernardino* **(J)**; it is dedicated to the popular preacher for whom the pulpit on the outside of the *Duomo* was built. Cross the grass and a minute later you are standing in front of the church. Have a good look at the façade (inside it's quite plain).

The marble reliefs on the façade were sculpted by Agostino di Duccio; they show scenes from the life of San Bernardino. The sculptor is not the Sienese Duccio di Buoninsegna, the famous medieval painter, but a Florentine artist of sufficient fame to have had an attempt at carving the block from which Michelangelo eventually sculpted David. When you look at the carvings, note the one where the preacher orders the Perugians (well known for their love of fighting) to burn their weapons. As the weapons burn, the Devil flies out of the fire. This has parallels to the "Bonfire of the Vanities" which occurred later on in Florence under the influence of the Dominican preacher Savonarola. Instead of weapons, the Florentines burnt their luxury items.

Leave the church and return the way you came, after 2 minutes, you pass *Via della Siepe* on your left. Ahead, you can see a large tower; these were common in medieval Italian cities and were the fortified houses of the aristocracy. As the merchant classes became more powerful, cities began to control the surrounding countryside. The aristocratic families found themselves owing allegiance to the new city-states.

0:49 Fortified towers within the walls of a city, especially when owned by powerful families with their own interests to pursue, presented too much of a threat to the new rulers. Most were pulled down, if you visit the *National Gallery of Umbria* after the walk, there is a fresco of the *Perugia* skyline which shows many of these towers (the same fresco which depicts the *Etruscan Arch* without the Renaissance loggia). One minute later you pass beside the base of the tower, continue walking up the street and 6 minutes beyond this, you pass under an arch and emerge back onto the *Corso Vannucci* **(C)**.

Galleria Nazionale dell' Umbria (National Gallery of Umbria)

0:56 Now it's time for more art. The *Galleria Nazionale dell' Umbria* (open daily 0900-1900, closed on the first Monday of each month) is housed within the *Palazzo dei Priori* and contains more work by Perugino, as well as altarpieces by Fra Angelico and Piero della Francesca. Turn left onto the *Corso Vannucci* and almost immediately, turn left again through the main entrance to the *Palazzo dei Priori* (the Gothic arch you passed earlier in the walk).

Walk straight on to the back of the building and you will find the ticket office through an entrance on your right. The ticket office for the museum is located here, well away from the gallery, which is located on the third floor. Once you have your ticket, you need to get to the gallery, there is a small lift near the ticket office or you can use the stairs near the entrance.

For those seriously interested in the development of Umbrian Art and its Sienese influences (many of the painters who worked at Assisi were Sienese), the first rooms display medieval art. I don't tend to linger here, I get a little bored looking at Crucifixions and paintings of the Madonna con Bambino, but feel free to take your time.

In room VIII, you will find an altarpiece by Fra Angelico (the museum uses his other name; "Beato Angelico"). Although he was a Renaissance painter, he was still influenced by the late medieval style, combining the newly mastered perspective with gold leaf and flowery backgrounds.

In room XI, you will find a sculpture of the Madonna and Child by Agostino di Duccio, the artist who carved the façade of the *Oratorio di San Bernardino.* The Madonna, especially, is surprisingly modern in style.

Turn around and you are confronted with, what in my opinion, is the museum's greatest masterpiece, an altarpiece from the church of St. Antony di Padua by Piero della Francesca. Piero della Francesca was a mathematician and his paintings demonstrate his interest in perfect perspective. He was a teacher of Perugino and you might notice his influence in Perugino's paintings further on in the Gallery. The Tuscans and Umbrians both like to include him amongst their painters because the town where he lived, Borgo Sansepolcro, once Umbrian, was sold by the Pope and became part of Tuscany.

In room XV, there is a series of eight paintings from Perugino's workshop on the left and another, larger painting on the right. The paintings on the left show the miracles performed by San Bernardino di Siena, the popular preacher. The painting on the right, an Adoration of the Magi, painted around 1470, shows a much younger Perugino than the one you saw earlier, staring straight out of the crowd.

In room XXI, the walls are frescoed with scenes from the siege of *Perugia* by the Goths. Although the siege took place in AD 547, the cityscape is decidedly medieval. Note the *Etruscan Arch* minus the Renaissance loggia and the numerous fortified towers within the city. The fresco shows Perugians having thrown a calf, stuffed with grain over the walls in a desperate last attempt to trick the Goths into thinking there is still plenty of food within the city. There is also a small painting by Perugino above a large altarpiece. Often overlooked by visitors due to its size and position on the wall, Christ in Pity (Imago Pietatis) is one of the best Perugino paintings in the Gallery.

The last room in the Gallery has several paintings by Perugino of varying quality. One painting shows the subject framed within a structure of simple design in order to demonstrate his skills of linear perspective (this is probably the influence of Piero della Francesca). Many of Perugino's paintings use this format; he had a vast workshop, which churned out commissions to order. He was not going to waste time developing a new arrangement for each client. The saccharine sweetness of the faces and camp male figures may not be entirely to modern tastes, but they appealed to the Pre-Raphaelite school of painters in England, who held Perugino's style in high regard.

Perugino was also one of the first painters to develop aerial, or "birds-eye" perspective. This technique dispenses with lines running towards a vanishing point; instead it tricks the brain into recognising distance by colouring the furthest objects and parts of the landscape in shades of blue. The next time you view any Tuscan or Umbrian landscape, look at the further hills and you will see that they appear to be a washed-out blue. Leonardo da Vinci went on to perfect this technique, he knew Perugino when they worked as pupils of Andrea Verrocchio in *Florence*.

When you have finished in the gallery, make your way back to the *Corso Vannucci*. You can wander the busy shopping area in the centre, have lunch, or make your way back to the car (turn right onto *Corso Vannucci* and retrace your steps).

Leaving *Perugia* by car can be as difficult as entering it. If it is your first visit, I recommend following signs to *Firenze* and *Roma* until you reach the Autostrada, these signs are the least likely to disappear and leave you lost in the one-way system.